IF YOU DO...
HAVE A DREAM

Ric –

I hope you enjoy reading my little effort as much as I enjoyed (a) living through this holiday and (b) setting it all down on paper to share with you.

Doug Powell

IF YOU DON' HAVE A DREAM

◆

LAUGHS, DISCOVERIES AND SURPRISES ON A FIRST VISIT TO THE U.S.A.

Doug Powell

iUniverse, Inc.
New York Lincoln Shanghai

IF YOU DON' HAVE A DREAM
LAUGHS, DISCOVERIES AND SURPRISES ON A FIRST VISIT TO THE U.S.A.

Copyright © 2006 by Doug Powell

All rights reserved. No part of this book may be used or reproduced by any means, graphic, electronic, or mechanical, including photocopying, recording, taping or by any information storage retrieval system without the written permission of the publisher except in the case of brief quotations embodied in critical articles and reviews.

iUniverse books may be ordered through booksellers or by contacting:

iUniverse
2021 Pine Lake Road, Suite 100
Lincoln, NE 68512
www.iuniverse.com
1-800-Authors (1-800-288-4677)

ISBN-13: 978-0-595-39216-2 (pbk)
ISBN-13: 978-0-595-83607-9 (ebk)
ISBN-10: 0-595-39216-4 (pbk)
ISBN-10: 0-595-83607-0 (ebk)

Printed in the United States of America

Contents

Introduction vii
DAY 1. 1
DAY 2. 7
DAY 3. 13
DAY 4. 23
DAY 5. 27
DAY 6. 30
DAY 7. 33
DAY 8. 37
DAY 9. 42
DAY 10. 47
DAY 11. 52
DAY 12. 55
DAY 13. 59
DAY 14. 63
DAY 15. 67
DAY 16. 70
DAY 17. 75
DAY 18. 81

DAY 19 86
DAY 20 89
DAY 21 93
DAY 22 98
DAY 23 102
DAY 24 105
DAY 25 108
DAY 26 112
DAY 27 115
DAY 28 118
DAY 29 122
DAY 30 126
DAY 31 128
DAY 32 131
DAY 33 137
DAY 34 139
DAY 35 142

Introduction

> You gotta have a dream—
> If you don' have a dream
> How you gonna have a dream come true?
>
> ('South Pacific')

I'm sure you don't need me to tell you that there is a tremendously strong American influence in so many aspects of our everyday British life. We see American films and TV programmes, we hear all about American sporting stars and politicians whilst American styles of clothing and food are gaining ground here and a number of American words have been added to our language. For many years I carried the idea in the back of my mind that one day I would like to visit America. I was curious to see for myself a little of this nation which has such far-reaching influence around the world. But somehow it seemed to be just a dream. Life was bustling past and it wasn't offering any chance to get across 'the pond'. Just a dream.

I have a cousin Maurice—everyone calls him Maury—whose wife, like mine, is named Mary. Maury and Mary are both American born and bred and live in Maryland, near to the border with Pennsylvania. They have been to England three times on holiday and have said to my Mary and me, "You must come over to the States some time and then we can show you our part of the world." It brought my dream a little closer but still nothing definite was arranged. One day, maybe.

Then came the point when our younger daughter, Elizabeth, emigrated to California with her husband Phil. He had the offer of an excellent job over there. Neither of them really wanted to leave England because their families and all their roots are, here but the offer was too good to refuse. So then they also started saying, "You must visit us in America"—and that's what finally motivated us.

First I must introduce the family group you are going to read about. I have mentioned MARY and MYSELF, ELIZABETH and PHIL. You will also meet our older daughter CATHERINE and her two daughters CHLOE and EMILY. They joined us in the latter part of the holiday. They live in Kent with Catherine's husband Paul, but pressure of work made it impossible for him to join us in America. And our son Andrew was also unable to be with us because he had just started a new job and could hardly begin by asking for time off.

Mary and I packed our bags, placed our two cats in a cattery (I don't think that was greeted with much enthusiasm!) and headed west. This is the story of our five-weeks holiday—one with a twofold mission. Firstly to visit relatives, cousin Maury and Mary and their family in Maryland, and then Elizabeth and Phil in California. But secondly, to see and experience this different world, to meet ordinary American people in their everyday homes and situations. To get away from all the sensational headlines and mix with folks who are just like ourselves. Are they really just like us? Well, why not come along with us and see for yourself?

DAY 1

It was on a late September afternoon that Mary and I flew from London to Washington. Our flight was due to leave Heathrow around lunchtime and so, calculating back from that time, we had booked a taxi to be at our house at 8 a.m. We reasoned that allowing for town centre traffic we would be in time to catch the 8.30 train from Southend Victoria to London. Southend-on-Sea is a little under forty miles from London and the journey takes an hour. We had chosen Victoria as that was the one local station where we would not have to negotiate staircases or bridges with heavy luggage.

In fact, our holiday got off to a good start. The taxi arrived a few minutes early, there was hardly any traffic on the roads and so we were at the station just in time to catch an earlier train, the 8.10. We felt that our planned schedule gave us plenty of time with no need to rush; nevertheless, it was nice to have the bonus of an extra twenty minutes in case we needed it.

And we did. We travelled across London by taxi, again to avoid problems with bulky luggage. But snag number one—there was quite a long queue for taxis at Liverpool Street station. And snag number two—the journey from Liverpool Street to Paddington took us through the Angel and Kings Cross district where there were delays due to road works. Our twenty minutes bonus soon disappeared together with some of the surplus time we had budgeted. And it was a painfully expensive ride because taxicab meters operate not on distance travelled but on time taken.

But at long last we breathed a sigh of relief as we trundled into Paddington station. Then we leisurely caught the Heathrow Express, a very comfortable train that in just fifteen minutes whisked us to the heart of the airport. From the station platform underground it is a lengthy walk through tunnels and up lifts to the terminal building and then through to the departure lounge. But we were not unduly worried. Time was still on our side.

This brought us to the next delay. There was a very long and slow-moving queue of passengers waiting to have their hand baggage checked. As we waited our turn we were astonished to see just how much some people were taking as hand baggage. As far as we know, the guiding principle is that it can be fitted into the space available above each seat on the aircraft. Indeed, one lady in front of us had so much 'hand baggage' that she needed a trolley to carry it. Finally we reached the front of the queue and passed through the x-ray machine. But in addition to the staff operating that, there was also one lady official just standing there and selecting a few passengers at random for closer scrutiny. Guess what—she called Mary aside for a thorough handbag search. Just our luck! She found nothing, of course, but it ate up still more minutes.

And so we moved into the departure lounge. Instant chaos! Half of it was boarded up during repair work and so everybody and everything was packed into the other half. From the indicator screens we noted our boarding gate number which, so it warned us, was a further twenty minutes' walk away. We decided to go and find exactly where it was and then return to the lounge. By the time we got back there our reservoir of surplus time was running rather low. In fact, we only had time for a brief look round and buy some sweets and a couple of magazines before our flight was announced.

The aircraft was a Boeing 747 jumbo jet. Both of us had flown on previous occasions but not in an aircraft of this size and so it was an interesting experience for us. There was one slight disappointment. We had reserved window seats but when we sat down we realised we were directly over a wing and so our view was somewhat limited. But not enough to spoil our enjoyment of the flight.

Departure time arrived; all the passengers were seated and then came an announcement from the captain. There was bad weather over Ireland and to avoid this Air Traffic Control were going to allocate an alternative flight path for us. This would, however, mean a delay before we would be taking off. So in the end we were about 40 minutes late starting our journey but there was one thing that made Mary and me laugh. Heathrow is a tremendously busy airport and when we finally moved onto the taxiway we were 14th in line to take off. Yes, 14th! At long last it came to our turn. Normally when an aircraft turns onto the runway there is a slight pause of thirty seconds or so—this is while the crew do their final, final check before opening up the engines. Not this time. Oh no. The moment the captain got onto that runway we were away, full speed ahead, within a couple of seconds. No messing about, it was all systems go. I suggested to Mary that maybe the captain lived in Washington and was anxious to get back home. Her reaction was, "Crumbs, I thought he was going to do a vertical take-off!"

I remember someone telling me that when he first flew he was surprised to find that above the clouds the sun always shines. I was reminded of that because it was a dull day at Heathrow with some drizzle, but within a few minutes of take-off we were in dazzling sunshine. And as it was on our side of the aircraft

Mary had to pull the window blind down. In a very short time we had reached our cruising level of 35,000 feet.

About an hour into the flight the cabin crew served lunch. Chicken, inevitably. I say 'inevitably' because people who fly frequently tell me that most airline meals are chicken in some form or other. But we thought it was a reasonable meal. We enjoyed it. (Jumping ahead for a moment, during our time in America we heard very little British news. But one snippet I picked up from a newspaper was that an English university was about to create a new research post. The subject to be covered is airline catering. I wondered whether regular travellers had campaigned for this, being fed up with 41 versions of chicken!)

After the meal we settled back to sample the in-flight entertainment. The 747 aircraft have separate TV monitors for each passenger and I managed to find a fascinating film which took us behind the scenes at Buckingham Palace. Mary had actually dozed off for about half an hour and when she woke up I told her which channel I was watching. I think she was just in time to catch the final thirty seconds and the credits!

Then we both switched over to another channel on which we could follow the progress of our flight assisted by maps, charts and weather reports. Not much longer now. We would very soon be setting foot on American soil.

Before reaching the States the cabin crew distributed Immigration forms to be completed by all non-American passengers. The usual questions—name, nationality, purpose of visit and so on. About a quarter of an hour later we were shown on one channel a guide to filling in these forms. But by then we had already done it and I bet most other passengers had as well. One point was interesting. Under Nationality Mary had written English. We had not collaborated in our answers and I had written British. The film giving the guidance showed U.K. as the correct answer. But nobody asked us any searching questions later.

There was a series of questions that amused me. They carried 'Yes/No' answers and it was perfectly obvious that everybody would answer 'No' to every one. So why on earth bother to ask the questions in the first place? "Are you, or have you ever been, a member of any illegal or subversive organisation?" I wondered whether to write "Yes—the Southend Organists' Association." "Are you bringing into the U.S.A. any drugs or banned substances?" Look, if I was, I would hardly tell the whole world, would I? "Are you importing any dangerous animals?" "Well, only my lifelong collection of blasphemous man-eating hard-drinking butterflies in this holdall." But no, I didn't write any of those answers. Customs and Immigration officers worldwide are not exactly noted for a strong sense of humour.

As we approached the coast the captain asked everyone to fasten his or her seat belts "as there seems to be some turbulence ahead". Heading west, we crossed the coast a little way north of Boston and as we then turned to south-west there was indeed a slight shuddering for a few moments. Is that all? D'you call that turbulence? We have known more jolting around in a car travelling along a bumpy road. In times past Mary and I have crossed the English Channel in much smaller aircraft. Now there you get *real* turbulence.

We continued down on the western side of New York, Philadelphia and Baltimore, but as we were so high we didn't actually see anything of those cities. The maps we were watching did not give the names of states but I think we passed over Massachusetts, Pennsylvania and Virginia. We may also have flown over the edge of Maryland—our final destination that day—but I'm not absolutely certain about that. As we made the final approach to Washington I can't say we dropped below the clouds because there weren't any clouds. It was a gloriously sunny day.

At this stage in Britain we were at the end of a disappointing summer. Lots of rain but only a few really hot days. So during the week before our holiday I had sent an e-mail to Maury. "I am sure you must be a man with considerable influence in the States and so I am looking to you to organise outstanding good weather for our visit."

When we landed we taxied to a parking bay some distance from the main terminal building and so we stepped from the aircraft into a transit bus. Golly, we really noticed the difference moving from the pressurised aircraft into the sauna-like atmosphere of the bus. But after a few minutes we were in the air-conditioned terminal building. That's when we made a strategic error. We came to a row of immigration desks with a queue at each. So we joined the one which seemed the shortest. Wrong!! It turned out to be moving much slower than the others (maybe other people had realised this and moved elsewhere) and so it was an eternity before we finally got through to the baggage reclaim area. So long, in fact, that all our fellow passengers on that flight had collected their luggage. The final two pieces—ours—had been taken off the carousel and placed to one side and it took us a few minutes to find them.

Thus at long last we arrived in the public area of the terminal building and there was Maury waiting to welcome us. We apologised for having kept him waiting so long. Had he wondered whether we had changed our minds and gone back to London? Then, as soon as we walked outside the building, the heat hit us again. He told us that after several rather indifferent days the temperature had suddenly shot up to 80 for our arrival. I congratulated him for this response to my e-mail.

His home is in Walkersville, a small community forty or so miles north of Washington. He drove us there with he and I sitting in the front seats and Mary in the back. Washington Dulles airport is some 20 miles to the west of the city (it's actually in the state of Virginia) but we did not have to go through the city centre on our journey. We skirted around the western suburbs. Nevertheless we had our first taste of an American rush hour because by then it was after 5 p.m. But as the American freeways (five lanes) are much wider than our British motorways (three lanes) the traffic kept moving at a reasonable pace.

There is so much space in America compared with Britain. The first thing I noticed was that those extra lanes make it possible to have slip roads and filter lanes at almost all junctions. But this means a somewhat involved arrangement for the traffic lights. To cope with this many, the lights are on poles that are projected across the road, giving separate signals for separate lanes. So the driver has to stay alert and remember which lane he is in and which way he wants to go. Another difference is that, apart from in the big cities, there are fewer roadside advertisement hoardings in America which presumably means less distractions for the driver. I think that's a good idea, especially on busy modern roads.

While we were still in the outskirts of Washington, Mary in the back seat saw something that amazed her. A truck drew up alongside us at the traffic lights. (In Britain we call them lorries but the American word is trucks.) Its bodywork was battered and corroded and there were holes right next to the engine. Surely it wasn't roadworthy, she thought, there's no way it should be on the road. She mentioned it to Maury and that started a conversation about the condition of American vehicles—to what extent do the authorities make checks? We told him about our M.O.T. tests in Britain and he was surprised to hear that every one of our vehicles over three years old has to undergo a thorough inspection every year, that this results in a certificate being issued and that without such a current certificate a vehicle cannot be taken onto any public road. He told us that no similar system exists in Maryland for private cars (though a number of other States have one) but some spot checks are carried out on commercial vehicles. However, these are carried out at the roadside and are a bit 'hit and miss' so it's not a very satisfactory system. The thinking seems to be that Americans treasure their freedom to drive on the nation's roads and their right to drive whatever vehicle they choose. This was the first illustration we had during our holiday of just what it means to American citizens when they speak so passionately about The Land Of The Free.

While Maury had come to meet us Mary (his Mary—we now had two of them) had stayed at home preparing a meal. One of their daughters, Jan, who also lives in Walkersville, was there with her to greet us. Being British, our first request was for a cup of tea. We then tucked into a very welcome (and substantial) meal and afterwards we all sat chatting long into the evening. Of course, travel is always a tiring experience and, in addition, by going westwards across the Atlantic, we had gained five hours. So by the time the clocks were showing 9 p.m. our bodies were telling us it was 2 a.m.; we had to call it a day. And what a fascinating day it had been.

One final point. Something I had heard years ago but had forgotten until now. In Britain light switches are down for on and up for off. In the States it's the other way round. I remembered it when I walked into our bedroom.

DAY 2

When children worldwide are taught history it is naturally the history of their own native lands. Here in Britain our youngsters also learn a certain amount of European history because over the centuries Britain (especially England and Scotland) has been affected quite dramatically by events on the continental mainland. So far as American history is concerned our British children know the story from Christopher Columbus (1492) up until the Declaration of Independence (1776) but very little after that. So they would be hard pressed to tell you much about the American Civil War (1861-65).

I think it is universally agreed that the greatest Englishman of the twentieth century was Winston Churchill—statesman, journalist, author, painter and the inspiring leader of the free world during the Second World War. As a writer, his greatest work was that masterpiece *A History Of The English-Speaking Peoples*, four volumes in length and acknowledged now as the finest reference work of its kind. In it he wrote at some length of the American Civil War. I am lucky enough to have my own copy and, yes, I *have* read it.

In the months leading up to our holiday I had borrowed books from our local library in order to read about those parts of the States we would be visiting. So I read several names that I knew were associated with that war. What I had not fully appreciated, however, was the extent to which the Civil War played a major part in the history of the areas around Walkersville.

For our first full day in the States we spent the morning just sitting quietly chatting—Maury, the two Marys and myself. Then Maury suggested, "If we have an early lunch there will be time this afternoon for us to show you Gettysburg. It's not too far away." Lunch incidentally included our first experience of potato bread. It was very tasty—we enjoyed it so much that we ate it several times while we were in Maryland and later, in California, introduced it to Elizabeth and Phil.

It was at Gettysburg in Pennsylvania that the Civil War reached its climax in July 1863. The Union army, commanded by General George G. Meade, clashed with the Confederate army under General Robert E. Lee. It was a horrific battle that lasted for three days involving some 67,000 soldiers. By the time it ended no less than 51,000 of them had been killed or seriously wounded.

Subsequently 17 acres of land were purchased in order to provide a proper burial ground and that has become the Gettysburg National Cemetery. It was dedicated on 19th November 1863 and at the ceremony President Abraham Lincoln made a short two-minutes speech which has become known as The Gettysburg Address. There were ten words in that speech that have become deeply ingrained in the American psyche: "Government of the people by the people for the people."

So after lunch Maury drove us all to Gettysburg mentioning along the way that we were just crossing the Mason-Dixon line, the boundary between Maryland and Pennsylvania. When we arrived it was very busy in spite of being midweek and it took him a few minutes to find a vacant space in the parking lot (that's American for car park). Mary and I were then a little surprised that he did not lock the car when we walked into the main building, the Visitor Centre. "You wouldn't do that in England." "Oh, it'll be all right," he told us quite confidently. (And it was.)

The Centre had numerous displays of pictures, weapons, maps, flags, etc., but we were not in there for very long. Then we went across the road to the Cemetery where we started taking photographs of each other. Considering how long Mary and I had been planning our holiday and how much we had been looking forward to it, people might think it a little strange that the first of our photographic souvenirs shows a cemetery. But this is no ordinary burial ground. The very name of Gettysburg commemorates a turning point in American history, a moment in time which established the path along which the United States are still travelling today. The National Cemetery is one focal point which is very special. There are several places in England which always give me an intense, almost overwhelming, feeling of the impact of history. I don't think I can adequately express that emotion in words. And even though I was an Englishman I could sense that Maury was experiencing the same feeling that afternoon at Gettysburg.

I have just written 'one focal point'. There is a second. A walk of roughly half a mile brought us to a large monument, which marks the actual spot where Abraham Lincoln stood when he delivered his Address. At the foot of the monument are some stone slabs on which are inscribed the full text of what he said. Again, a very special spot for all who have a deep sense of American history. Incidentally, as the Address was quite short (272 words to be precise) there used to be a story that he scribbled it out on the back of an envelope. But people who were with him at the time soon established that this was just a myth, a total invention, a little story which probably sounds good after a few beers!

Following an accident some time previously, Maury's Mary had difficulty in walking long distances and so she had waited for us on a park bench opposite the Visitor Centre whilst we three walked to the monument. We were taking pictures in turns, each of us photographing the other two. Then a man approached us. "Would you like a picture of the three of you together?" We accepted his offer with thanks and this proved to be just the first of several such offers while we were in the States. We have returned to England with warm memories of the great friendliness which we encountered throughout our visit to America.

Back at the Visitor Centre we met up with Mary again and Maury suggested that we visit the Eisenhower farm. This is a couple of miles away and visitors can only reach it via a shuttle bus service from the Visitor Centre. At that stage I didn't know if the farm had any special significance but I soon learned otherwise.

The name of Dwight D. Eisenhower was not really well known to the British public until late 1943. Born in Texas, he grew up in Kansas and chose a career in the U.S. Army. His school friends nicknamed him Ike and this name stayed with him throughout his life.

By 1943 the Allied forces had become strong enough to challenge the German, Italian and Japanese combination. 'Operation Overlord' was planned, to take place in June 1944, and General Eisenhower was named as Supreme Allied Commander. His orders were simple. "You will land in Europe and, proceeding to Germany, will destroy Hitler and all his forces." The success of the campaign brought about the end of World War Two.

On leaving the army he became President of Columbia University but was never really at ease there. (One of the guides during our visit explained it like this. When Ike told a soldier to do something the man would snap to attention, salute and shout YESSIR!!! When he told a professor to do something the reaction was sometimes, "Why?") In 1950 he and his wife Mamie purchased this farm just outside Gettysburg as their retirement home but in 1952 he was persuaded to run for President of the U.S.A.—and he won. So the farm became a kind of retreat home where he could take visiting heads of state. There he could work quietly and have private informal discussions away from the pressures of Washington.

He stepped down from the Presidency in 1961 and a few years later he and Mamie gifted their home and property to the U.S. government with the proviso that they lived the rest of their lives there. Ike died in 1969 and Mamie ten years later.

We found it interesting to see around the farmhouse, which still remains unchanged. The living room is, I felt, rather over-furnished. I agree with Ike. He rarely used the room because he considered it too stuffy. His favourite was the conservatory-style porch, looking out over a putting green and large garden. During our visit I picked up a leaflet giving information on different rooms and I think the comments about the master bedroom upstairs are worth repeating here.

> *Mamie believed that once a woman reached the age of 50 she was entitled to stay in bed until noon. She took advantage of that entitlement here in the master bedroom. She met with staff members, wrote correspondence and planned her social agenda, all while in bed propped up on pillows. After the General died she kept his side of the bed piled with books, stationery and candy so that it would not seem so empty.*

Back downstairs is a small room used as Ike's office and sparsely furnished with desk, chair, telephone and two bookshelves. I quote again from the leaflet.

> *The desk is a reproduction of one used by George Washington. The gift was made with pine boards recovered from the White House during its 1948/52 renovation. Eisenhower received a phone call here on 7th May 1960 informing him that the Soviet Union not only shot down the U-2 spy plane but also captured its pilot, Francis Gary Powers.*

I referred just now to Maury feeling that strong sense of history and here I experienced it myself as I stood in that little office and gazed at the telephone. I remember the Gary Powers incident and the shattering effect it had on the western world. Here in front of me was the very phone that brought the terrible message.

And I felt it again a few minutes later as we stood on the paved area outside the front door. Our guide said that as a contrast from the porch at the rear of the house Ike would at times bring his famous guests here and they would sit relaxing. I realised that I was standing on the very same spot where before me Winston Churchill, Charles de Gaulle, Konrad Adenauer and Nikita Kruschev had enjoyed this same view. The superb lines of Norwegian spruce trees, the rolling fields beyond and away on the horizon the famous Blue Ridge Mountains. There are moments in life when the sheer enormity of history can make a mere human being feel very small and insignificant.

After seeing inside the building we then walked around the immediate grounds. Ike had run the farm with partners, producing corn, wheat and hay. There had also been a dairy herd and some prize-winning Angus cattle. In the centre of the garden is a huge flagpole and when Ike was here the Presidential standard was flown. After he retired from the White House he was reinstated with the honorary rank of General and for the rest of his life the General's five star flag flew proudly in this garden.

Not far from the front of the main building is a two-roomed guesthouse. It is what we might call a summerhouse and is in the style of the early settlers, complete with porch and railing. Quite fascinating.

My dictionary describes a surrey as 'a light two-seater four-wheeled carriage' and years ago the surrey was immortalised in song. I had travelled to the States wanting to see the real America, to absorb myself in the atmosphere of the nation. Walking around the grounds we came to the small garage, which, we discovered, had originally been the chicken house. And look what was standing there! Yes, in real life, a genuine Surrey With A Fringe On Top. Oh great—now this really is the kind of thing I had come to America to see.

Eventually it was time to get back onto the bus and travel back to the Visitor Centre. As we did so I pondered over what we had just seen. I (and, I think, Mary) had gone to the farm not expecting anything very special. A farm is a farm is a farm. But what an absolute gem it had turned out to be. Packed full of modern history and reviving memories of the world's leading men during my younger days. I had just trodden where they had trod. It also brought home to me the great esteem in which Americans hold their countrymen and women who have served in the armed forces. In Britain we respect (at least, I hope we do!) our O.A.P's—old age pensioners—and in recent times this title is slowly being changed to senior citizens. In America these people are already known as seniors and many times during our holiday I noticed that privileges and concessions are available to 'seniors and veterans'. The impression I get is that all those who have served the U.S. in the armed forces are regarded as having earned the right to privileges under the title of veterans. In our own country, by contrast, the only ex-servicemen and women we seem to hold in special regard are those who have been wounded or disabled in action. To them we offer an additional pension but nothing more.

Travelling the previous evening from Washington to Walkersville I had been very impressed by the lovely trees along the way. Miles of beautiful forestry. I noticed it again as we returned now from Gettysburg. The state of Maryland alone has approximately 4,000 square miles of woodland. Visiting America in late September we had expected to see lots of autumn colours, but in fact everything was still decked in glorious shades of green. Obviously summer was still far from over in this part of the world. Something else which caught Mary's attention was a great expanse of sweetcorn crops not yet harvested. Was this not rather late, she enquired? The reply was that it had been a wonderful summer that had produced bumper crops. Up to now there simply hadn't been sufficient time to gather them all in. The farmers were still working at full stretch to finish the harvesting before the weather finally changed. What a difference from the miserable summer we had left behind us in England.

A quiet, relaxing evening brought to a close our first full day in America. We had thoroughly enjoyed every minute of it and were now looking forward to something we knew was going to be really special on the following day.

DAY 3

Up with the lark today. We had to be out of the house by 6.45 at the latest.

Mornings in America start earlier than for us in Britain. We regard 9 a.m. as the magic hour when everything comes to life. But in the States many offices and some shops are under way at 8 a.m. So are schools—indeed a number of schools begin at 7.30. This all means that the morning rush hour in America begins soon after 6 a.m., an hour or so earlier than in Britain. Today we were going to visit the White House, which should normally involve a one-hour journey. But to be there by 8.30 and allowing for the rush hour, we had to be on our way well before 7.0.

Perhaps I first ought to show how the governments of our two nations compare:

BRITAIN	U. S. A.
Parliament	Congress
House of Lords	The Senate (100 members—2 from each state)
House of Commons	House of Representatives (435 members at present)
Prime Minister (who is the leader of the majority party in the Commons)	President (elected by the people at separate elections)
Conservative Party	Republican Party
Labour Party	Democrat Party
Liberal Democrat Party	(No established third party)
A government, once elected, can choose to serve for any period up to a maximum of five years	All members of the House of Representatives are elected for two years

We were visiting the White House (the President's official Mansion) and the Capitol (the government building) as guests of Ellen Bartlett. Her husband, the

Hon. Roscoe J. Bartlett, was one of the senior Congressmen and I think that made him the equivalent of a British Cabinet Minister. We didn't actually meet him that day and I'll explain the reason for that later. Mary and I were very lucky in that the Bartletts are personal friends of Maury and Mary and were able to produce this special occasion for us. We knew in advance that our day would involve a lot of walking and as that gave problems for Maury's Mary she decided, with disappointment, to remain at home. So there were seven in our party—Maury, Jan and Megan (his two youngest daughters), Patrick (a grandson), Ellen Bartlett and Mary and myself. We two, being visitors from England, seemed to be treated as guests of honour, which was all very flattering.

During my pre-holiday studies I had read that there are public guided tours of the White House that are free of charge and are tremendously popular—to such an extent that queues begin forming at daybreak or even earlier; intending visitors should be prepared to queue for two hours at the very least. (By the way, I'm writing in English now. Americans don't know the word 'queue'. They simply call it a line.)

All along the road outside the White House the few parking spaces are very strictly reserved for senior officials and special guests. Ellen Bartlett had obviously done her homework and the two passes for Pennsylvania Avenue, which she had obtained, were worth their weight in gold. Oh, what a lovely, lovely moment it was when our two cars glided along this world-famous road, stopped to one side of the White House, the seven of us got out and strolled casually towards the building, past all those people who had been standing there for Heaven knows how long. They must have wondered who on earth we were.

The next moment was glorious as well. Standing in the doorway were three members of the Secret Service (that's the Presidential security staff). As we reached them Ellen said, "This is my party—there are seven of us." They appeared only mildly interested and so she added, "I am Mrs. Bartlett. My husband is Ros Bartlett." What a dynamic reaction. "Yes, MA'AM!! Good morning, MA'AM!! This way, MA'AM!!" We were all ushered in; she mentioned in passing that Mary and I were guests from England and it made us both feel like visiting royalty. It continued like that for the rest of the day. Ellen merely had to announce herself as Ros Bartlett's wife and doors opened everywhere.

In the reception area we were all invited to sign the Visitors' Book. Mary suggested that I sign for both of us but I wouldn't agree. "No, you do it yourself and then you can tell everybody that your signature is in the White House Visitors' Book." So there they are, our two signatures for future generations to admire—'Doug Powell, Southend-on-Sea, England' and on the next line 'Mary

Powell, Southend-on-Sea, England'. I wonder if our Queen and Prince Philip will one day pay another state visit to the President and, as they have previously, will sign that book. If she then nonchalantly glances back over a few pages she might say, "Oh Philip, look—Doug and Mary were here the other day." (Well, it's a nice dream.)

The system seems to be that private tours start at 8.30 a.m. and are followed by the public ones from 10.0 onwards. The reason is that the buffer of an hour and a half allows time for the private ones to take in parts of the White House, which are not then included in the public tours. For a start, the general public don't sign the Visitors' Book.

There were several people waiting and so the Secret Service officers divided us all up into three groups and we seven were careful to ensure that we all stayed together. Each private tour is escorted by a Secret Service officer acting as a guide, whereas the general public get no such assistance. They are merely allowed just twenty minutes in which to see certain designated rooms, watched closely by Secret Service officers posted along the way.

We were taken firstly out to the Jacqueline Kennedy Garden, which is not on the public tour. This secluded area on the east side of the building remained somewhat neglected until Jacqueline became the First Lady. She had it cultivated extensively and nowadays it serves primarily as a quiet and informal reception area away from all the media attention. Our guide seemed unsure whether the President was in residence or not. "I thought he is away, but on second thoughts I'm not so sure." Our enquiries later elicited that he was there in the building at the same time as us but was preparing to fly to Canada later that day.

We were then shown around the various rooms on the Ground Floor. (On entering the building the general public are directed straight upstairs to the State Floor.) One which I particularly remember was the China Room. From the earliest days Presidents received government funds from which to purchase state china and we saw beautiful examples on display in a number of cabinets. But as the years passed some items became cracked during use or slightly damaged and it was agreed that these could be auctioned or sold off, the proceeds being put towards the cost of new china. But eventually in 1901 along came President Theodore Roosevelt's wife who strongly opposed this practice. She insisted that any damaged china must be broken up and scattered in the nearby Potomac River.

Upstairs on the State Floor we walked along the wide, impressive main hallway, which is known as the Cross Hall and is covered with a gorgeous deep-pile red and gold carpet. It leads into the large East Room, lavishly decorated in gold and white. This must be the best-known part of the White House because it is seen around the world regularly on television news programmes. They set up microphones in that room when Presidents make announcements. So nowadays when Mary and I see those items on TV we smile smugly and say, "We walked along that lovely red carpet. And look, George Bush is standing exactly where we stood. If they would just turn the cameras slightly to the right we would be able to see that superb grand piano over by the window." Because it is quite large this room has been the scene of Presidential receptions and the weddings of three Presidents' daughters. It is also where Richard Nixon made his speech resigning the Presidency in 1974 after the Watergate scandal.

Then on to the Green Room. I mention this as it used to have one special feature. When Thomas Jefferson was America's third President he used it as a dining room and had a revolving door fitted. This door had trays on one side. The idea was that staff could place food on the trays and then revolve the door. So those inside the room could obtain their food in privacy without being interrupted. A unique feature, but it was scrapped when this room was refurbished in 1971.

The only other room I'll mention (after all, this is not intended to be a comprehensive guide book) is the State Dining Room. What caught my eye was the inscription by John Adams carved into the mantel:

> I PRAY HEAVEN TO BESTOW THE BEST OF BLESSINGS ON THIS HOUSE AND ON ALL THAT SHALL HEREAFTER INHABIT IT. MAY NONE BUT HONEST AND WISE MEN EVER RULE UNDER THIS ROOF.

Very noble sentiments and deserving of respect from all of us. But I couldn't help feeling that they are a little ironic, remembering that several Presidents have been involved in scandals, either political or financial or moral. We must just hope for better things in future.

One room on the Ground Floor has been made into a book and gift shop and before we left I purchased an excellent book about the White House. Later I asked all of our seven to sign the flyleaf—it now makes a lovely souvenir of the day.

Walking back to the cars, Maury and Ellen were just behind me and they were talking about Pennsylvania Avenue. That part of it immediately in front of the White House is pedestrianised but I gather that this is a comparatively recent move. They both remember the avenue before the change. I thought nothing of it at the time but some two weeks later, when I was in California, I read an article in a newspaper. Here are some extracts from that.

> *Way back when the executive mansion was first built, the Founding Fathers determined that the president should never be mistaken for a king. They wanted to make certain that his official residence be as far removed from the trappings of royalty as possible. For all of its 200-year existence, the White House remained just a house on a street with a number. Americans always could walk or ride by this edifice of freedom and truly feel it belonged to them. Throughout much of its history there weren't even fences or gates. Every president withstood the pleadings of those charged with his safety to take the ultimate step that would change the very nature of the residence—closing off the broad thoroughfare in front to motor traffic.*
>
> *After the bombing of the federal courthouse in Oklahoma City President Clinton acceded to the wishes of the security experts and did the unthinkable. He endorsed a plan diverting as many as 20,000 vehicles a day onto other already busy streets. It turned "everyman's" residence into a palace, the most drastic move short of also ending foot traffic on the avenue. A plan has now been proposed which would halve the number of lanes, enough to allow the passage of automobiles but not trucks, and provide pedestrian footbridges across. The Secret Service is apparently opposed to the idea.*
>
> *Of course the safety of the president is paramount. On the other hand he was ill-advised when he accepted the most drastic action available. The proposal to re-open seems utterly reasonable.*

The words 'Land Of The Free' are ingrained deep on the heart of every American, man, woman or child. We British are also very proud of our freedom but somehow we don't seem so passionate about it as the Yanks. Freedom is all-important to them and seems to override every other consideration. I have written earlier about their right, their freedom to drive whatever type of vehicle they wish. They defend their freedom to decide, state by state, how public money is allocated. Some aspects of self-expression are carried to almost extreme lengths in the name of freedom of speech. So after reading that article I could now understand that it was very important to American citizens that they *must* have the freedom to drive their cars past the White House. Merely walking past was insufficient. I don't think we English would take it to heart to the same extent if the road in front of Buckingham Palace were permanently closed to vehicles. (Well, of course it is closed temporarily when we have state occasions. And I've not heard of anyone kicking up a fuss.) This was the type of comparison between our two peoples which I found interesting, what I had come to America to find out.

Let's get back to the story. We drove the short distance, roughly one mile, to the Capitol and Ellen led us into the private car park. For the rest of the time we were all her personal guests and this is when Mary and I realised that the Bartlett name carried considerable influence. Members of the public can tour the Capitol but I think they are only allowed in the public galleries of the House of Representatives in the south wing and of the Senate in the north wing. To get from one to the other they pass through the Rotunda, that huge domed hall which dominates the Washington skyline, watched closely by Secret Service officers every inch of the way. But Ellen took us all over the place—she was in her element.

As I understand it, the House of Representatives had the previous afternoon been debating an amendment to their annual budget. I think they wanted to transfer some surplus money from one heading to another. Their decision had been taken to the President in the evening and so today they would be meeting to sort out all the precise details of the transfer. But for some reason (possibly some party political point-scoring) the President had refused to sign the necessary authorisation. In America, unlike Britain, the head of state has the power of veto. So today there was nothing for the House to discuss and thus no session. Consequently Ellen's husband was out of town taking advantage of this opportunity to deal with constituency matters.

It meant that Ellen was able to tell the Secret Service men at the door leading into the Chamber who she was and in we went. She has a sense of humour and throughout the day kept reminding everyone of the occasion in 1814 when British marines set fire to the White House. "This is Doug and Mary. They are my guests from England. They burnt down the White House, you know." In the Chamber we all sat in the front seats while she explained the layout and the procedures of the House. It is the largest legislative chamber in the world and is where Presidents give the annual State of the Union address. It was a fantastic privilege to be able to sit there—just like sitting on the front benches of our own House of Commons in London. Looking up, I saw two groups of 'ordinary' tourists in the public gallery gazing down at us. Huh, hoi-polloi, I thought!

The Rotunda in the very heart of the building is quite awe-inspiring. A circular hall, 96 feet wide, capped by that massive dome 180 feet high. All round the hall, immediately beneath the dome, is a frieze depicting historical events from Christopher Columbus through to the Wright brothers' flight at Kitty Hawk. On the circular walls there are eight immense oil paintings and Ellen pointed to one which shows the presentation of the Declaration of Independence with all the signatories gathered round. She indicated one young man towards the edge of the group. "That was my husband's great-great-great-uncle." No wonder there was a note of pride in her voice.

Although the general public see inside the Rotunda, they cannot do what we did next. Thanks to Ellen we stepped outside onto the balcony, which is high above the street, and from here we had a wonderful view across the eastern half of the city—Pennsylvania Avenue, The Mall and away in the distance the towering Washington Monument dominating the skyline. At 555 feet high that marble obelisk is the tallest masonry tower in the world. We were very lucky because for some time leading up to a few weeks before our visit it was shrouded in tarpaulins as it received a thorough cleaning. Now sparkling white on this bright sunlit morning, it was quite breathtaking. The whole view of this grand city was really awe-inspiring and I felt very privileged knowing that only a few people are allowed to stand on this balcony. This was emphasised by a burly Secret Service officer closing the double door quite firmly behind us when we moved back inside the building.

Arriving at the Senate Chamber we found that they were in session and so we sat in the public gallery for about five minutes. It was quite an experience to be there at the very heart of government of one of the world's foremost nations. Only a handful of Senators were present and the one speaking was paying tribute to some prominent citizen in his own area who had recently died. To me, without wishing to be in any way disrespectful, the most interesting aspect of the Senate was that this was the chamber where Bill Clinton stood and faced impeachment proceedings in connection with the Monica Lewinsky episode.

Senators and Representatives have their own offices but these are located in separate buildings across the road from the Capitol. To reach them there is an underground railway operating a shuttle service. Ellen wanted us to see her husband's office and so we had a ride on the railway. A most impressive office, because the walls were literally covered with certificates, diplomas and awards. They covered engineering, farming and other industries—he was obviously a highly talented man who over the years had worked very hard for the people he represented and thus earned their respect and gratitude. Most memorable was the certificate showing that he had received the Jefferson Award for services to America's space research programme. I was a little disappointed that we didn't have the chance to meet him.

Ellen so enjoyed showing us around that we had to remind her it was lunchtime. So back on the underground railway again, this time making a beeline for the staff cafeteria. There Mary and I became temporarily separated from the others. It was because we saw on the menu 'grilled ham and cheese sandwiches'. That sounded tasty and so I asked for 'grilled ham sandwich twice, please'. Unfortunately, what I didn't realise was that there is no word 'twice' in the American language. I was told later that what I should have asked for was 'grilled ham sandwich two times'. This caused a delay during which the others went ahead of us. And then at the cash desk the lady was so impressed with Mary's English accent that she insisted on having a conversation with her. I felt slightly embarrassed because a queue (sorry, line) of Capitol staff was building up behind us, all of them using up their limited lunch break time. So I tried gently to move things along a bit by asking the lady how much I owed for the lunch we were buying. All that happened was that she looked across at me open-mouthed and gasped, "Ah gee—he tocks like thett as whale!"

After lunch Ellen continued showing us almost every corridor and painting in the building. Everywhere she was treated with deference and we received special greetings from all the staff as visitors from England (even though we burnt down the White House, you know). Turning into one corridor we met three men just coming out of an office and the first one said "Good afternoon" to me. "Good afternoon," I replied, and we all continued on our various ways. A moment later Ellen asked if I had recognised him—he was Dick Cheney. Good Heavens—the Vice-President himself!! There are 276 million people in the States and he was number two in the whole nation. That made him one of the most powerful men in the western world. And I had spoken personally to him without realising who he was. Still, there are two sides to every story, aren't there? He hadn't realised who *I* was. If he ever finds out then maybe he will always boast to his friends, "One day I spoke to Doug from England. He burnt down the White House, you know."

Finally Ellen had exhausted the Capitol (and everybody else!). We were almost on our knees having seen quite literally all there was to see. Time to return to the parking lot and make our way home. But before we say goodbye to Ellen I must tell you about the car which she and her husband owned—a Toyota Prism that cost $ 20,000 (around £ 14,000 in our money). A hybrid vehicle, which operated on both petrol and electricity. It was computer-controlled and the idea was that it ran on fuel whilst the battery was charging up. When it was fully charged the computer automatically switched over to electricity and this continued until the battery ran down. Then the computer switched back to the fuel and the whole process started again. Ellen told us that a few weeks previously her husband Ros had used the car for a very long journey and on that day he had averaged 98 miles for each gallon of petrol. I suspect that a similar car in Britain would cost far more than £14,000.

Driving out of Washington we made use of a system which cannot exist in Britain because we simply don't have the space. On many American freeways one lane, on the offside, is reserved for H.O.V. That's high-occupancy vehicles. Only vehicles with a minimum of two occupants may use that lane. Not only does it help to speed things up during the busy periods but also it is an incentive for people to share transport. As we sped along I saw how congested the other lanes were. It really does highlight just how many drivers travel alone. No wonder we hear so much nowadays about pollution and global warming. Possibly the hybrid vehicle is one possible answer to the problem—but first of all it would be necessary to bring down the price to within the range of ordinary working people.

◆　　◆　　◆

While we are thinking about Washington it is worth adding a few sentences about the origins of the city.

When the original 13 states banded together their first disagreement was over just where the capital of the new U.S.A. would be. Each state wanted to nominate one of its own cities. So up until 1790 the new government held its meetings in Baltimore, Philadelphia, York, Lancaster, Princeton, Annapolis, Trenton and New York. Indeed, one prominent spokesman suggested that a statue of George Washington, which had been built, should perhaps be mounted on wheels so that it could follow the government wherever the meetings were held!

At long last a solution was put forward. The new capital would not belong to any one state. An area on the eastern bank of the River Potomac was identified which was actually 70% in Maryland and 30% in Virginia. Each state was willing to hand over the land in order that a brand new city could be built. It was agreed that the city would be named Washington in honour of George Washington, the first President, and the land on which it stood would be called the District of Columbia in honour of Christopher Columbus. So to this day the capital is always referred to as Washington D.C.

Some fifty years later, in 1846, following a request from Virginia, the area of land originally surrendered by them was handed back.

One district in today's city is named Foggy Bottom. (Yes it is, honestly, I can show you on the map.) It's because at that spot there were originally marshes which back in the steamy 18th century summers were havens of malaria. But from that there sprang up stories that the entire city has been built on swamps which are still slowly sinking today. It's not true—the land as a whole was mostly farmland or forest.

A Frenchman, Major Pierre Charles l'Enfant, was appointed to design the new city, but whilst his work was brilliant he himself managed to upset a great many people. He angered landowners in particular because his design spread beyond the area originally specified and he started seizing land without offering any compensation. As a result he was sacked in 1792 after just one year. For that year's work the government offered him $ 2,500, which he refused to accept. Instead he sued for $ 100,000—and lost. The rest of his life just went downhill and he was declared bankrupt several years before his death. It seems so strange that after designing one of the most magnificent cities in the world his remains now lie somewhere in an un-named pauper's grave.

Oh, by the way, on the subject of Washington—that bit about Mary and me burning the White House down. Let's get the record straight, if you don't mind!

Originally the president's home was known as the Presidential Mansion. When the Napoleonic War broke out America was neutral and was in fact trading with both sides, Britain and France. This upset the British who eventually declared war on America. One night in August 1814 a group of British marines sailed up river, landed at Washington and under cover of darkness set fire to the Mansion and several other government buildings. The inside of the Mansion was completely gutted but at that moment a heavy rainstorm started. The force of the rain extinguished the flames, thus saving the outside of the building. As part of the repair work the outer walls were all painted white in order to conceal the marks of the fire. Thus it got the nickname of the White House and this soon became accepted as the official name.

But I think I managed to convince people that I was not around at the time.

DAY 4

This was a gentle, restful day following all the activity and excitement of the previous day. Maury and Mary used the opportunity to show us around their neighbouring city of Frederick. It has a population of some 45,000 and if my calculations are correct is just about 3,700 miles from Southend. (A little too far to swim.) Surrounded by rolling farmlands and rugged mountains, it is the market centre of rich agricultural country, a city of two distinct parts. The modern section is quite pleasing and we saw some very smart houses set in attractive residential roads. But in the city centre, around the Courthouse Square area, the older buildings retain clear signs of their Germanic origins. Mary and I were particularly impressed with the 19th century colonial-style houses with wooden verandas at the front. Very reminiscent of the early settlers.

The city was established in 1745 by Palatinate Germans and is named after Frederick, the 6th Lord Baltimore. It soon achieved a measure of notoriety because prior to the American War of Independence local judges committed one of the first acts of colonial protest. They permitted unstamped commercial and legal documents in clear defiance of Britain's 1765 Stamp Act.

When Americans make reference to historical buildings they mean those that are around two hundred years old. After all, the U.S.A. was only born in 1776. By contrast we in Britain have many buildings that date back a thousand years. But we need to be careful not to give any impression of our being condescending when the Yanks proudly show us their oldest landmarks.

As Maury drove through the city he zigzagged from street to street and I lost my sense of direction. But as he pointed out landmarks I recognised several names which I had been reading about previously. There was the Schifferstadt Architectural Museum which was built in 1756 and is the oldest dwelling still surviving. We passed the Taney House and Key Museum. Brothers-in-law Roger Brooke Taney and Francis Scott Key were two solicitors in partnership and each has a niche in history. It was Supreme Court Justice Taney who administered the oath of office to President Abraham Lincoln. He was also the author of the Dred Scott Decision, which stated that blacks had no constitutional rights. Francis Key used to write poetry in his spare time and he wrote one piece under the title 'The

Star-Spangled Banner'. Little could he realise that much later, in the twentieth century, it would be set to music and adopted as America's national anthem.

We passed the Mount Olivet Cemetry, which is where Francis Scott Key is buried. Next, Maury pointed out All Saints, the only Episcopal Church in Frederick and this was of interest to us because we had already said we would like to attend a church service on the following day, being a Sunday. The Episcopal Church is the American counterpart of our Church of England.

From the outside we also had a brief look at Fort Detrick, though it might not be regarded as a 'tourist spot'. Important in its own way to the U.S. military, although hardly attractive. It is the government's study and storage facility for chemical and germ research and provides a considerable source of employment in the city.

Along one road I could easily have missed a small, modest brick cottage had Maury not indicated it. This was the true-to-life reconstruction of the Barbara Fritchie House. During the American Civil War this lady was a staunch supporter of the North and one day, when she was 95 years old, Confederate troops led by General Stonewall Jackson were marching past her home. Stubbornly she waved a Union flag, ignoring the soldiers' orders to stop. The old lady even defied the General himself and so, presumably to avoid an embarrassing situation, he let her continue flying it. That, I understand, is the gist of the story, but many years later John Greenleaf Whitter wrote a poem 'Barbara Fritchie'. I suspect that he added a few embellishments and this has established the story in romantic American folklore.

Our special attention was drawn to an office block downtown. (Americans refer to all town centres and city centres as downtown.) The fascia over the corner office read 'Richard Hassett & Co. Certified Accountants.' Richard (or Rick) is the eldest of Maury and Mary's children and we would be meeting him on the following day. I was looking forward to that, as I had recently retired from my own career as an accountant.

Then we moved on to what Mary and I will always remember as the most amazing feature in the whole of Frederick. A canal runs through the city and we parked the car near a bridge. What a beautiful stone bridge, we thought, as we walked towards it. How wonderfully preserved. "Touch it," suggested Maury. Imagine our astonishment when we did and then realised that it is in fact just plain cement facing. That's how the bridge was built, but the story is that in 1993 a local artist, William M. Cochran, decided that it was much too unattractive and so he painted it. Without doubt it is the most brilliant example of external painting that I have ever seen or could hope to see. He has shown stonework complete with crevices and shading, lichen and moss growing in some of the cracks, even a small doorway. It is totally convincing, so much so that even when you are standing a few inches away you would still declare that it is a stone bridge. We just had to take some photographs of it which we now show to all our friends here in England and say, "Look at this plain cement bridge."

By now it was almost time for lunch but there was just one more call. We had seen hardly any shops in the city and so we were taken to the Francis Scott Key Mall. To us it was very reminiscent of the Lakeside complex a few miles from our home back in Southend. Four main department stores and 85 smaller retail outlets. (Oh, here's a quick elocution lesson for you. Brits and Yanks both use the word 'mall'. But whereas we make it rhyme with 'shall', they make it rhyme with 'shawl'.) There was one incident which caught me unawares when we went into a bookstore. In Britain, V.A.T. is set by the government and is at the same rate throughout the whole country. Prices displayed in shops include that tax. In America there is no V.A.T. but they have a Sales Tax; this is set by each individual state and thus varies from one to another. And most, but not all, prices displayed are *before* tax is added. So if you are not brilliant at mental arithmetic you cannot always be absolutely sure of the exact price you will have to pay until the assistant tells you.

That's what happened to me. I selected a book, noted the price printed on the cover and offered that amount to the cashier. But the cash register was asking me for a little more and I suddenly remembered about the sales tax. Fortunately I had enough small change in my pocket as otherwise I might have had to change a twenty-dollar bill in order to cover the few extra cents. And for the rest of our time in America I knew what to expect.

So far we had been blessed with lovely weather to start our holiday but in that part of America their weather is sometimes similar to Britain's. So we were not surprised to hear that rain was on the way. After our brief tour of Frederick we spent the afternoon at home as although it was still dry it had turned a little gloomy. The four of us did a lot of talking during those few days in Maryland. We compared our two countries, we dealt with all the matters concerning race relations, political incompetence, cultural differences, problems with Europe and the Middle East. All rather serious, I suppose, but nevertheless quite intriguing to discover just how our two major nations vary in their approach to this modern era. By the time we finished we were on the point of telling our Prime Minister and their President to pack up and go home. Don't worry, lads—Maury and Doug are quite ready and capable of running the western world. But unfortunately it hasn't happened—somebody must have forgotten to tell the western world.

During the afternoon I had my first experience of speaking to an American over the telephone. Talking to people face to face I had found no problem at all with our varying accents but it was not so easy over the phone. It happened when I contacted the airline at Washington airport, the usual formality call just to confirm our booking for the flight to Los Angeles and confirm the departure time. It should have been quite straightforward but I'm afraid I had to ask the lady a couple of times to repeat what she had just said. I hope she didn't think I was incredibly stupid.

It was back to Frederick again in the evening as Maury had booked a table at a restaurant which he and Mary sometimes visit. Normally they go there on a Friday evening but this time with us it was Saturday. So the restaurant was quite crowded, but obviously the proprietor knows his regular customers and he had a good table for us. It was a very pleasant evening. Mary (that's my Mary) and I are both fond of salmon and when we saw that on the menu we both chose it for our main course. But back came apologies. As it was such a busy evening there was only one portion of salmon left. I let Mary take it and instead I chose boiled shrimps. When they arrived never in my life have I seen such huge shrimps. I would have described them as king prawns at the very least. They were delicious.

All restaurants are the same, aren't they? As the number of customers builds up so does the amount of conversation. That means that people start talking a little louder in order to make themselves heard. The volume rises steadily. Actually this particular restaurant was not as bad as some I have known but even though I was not in any way trying to listen to neighbours' conversations, it was impossible not to hear fragments. One word was repeated regularly. Arr-sm. Well, to my English ear that's what it sounded like. What they were in fact saying was 'awesome'. I should have mentioned that our visit to Maryland coincided with the Olympic Games and the U.S.A. was winning medals by the bucketful. Their athletes were certainly putting on some great performances and everyone back in the States was saying that their men and women were arr-sm.

When we had finished our meal the proprietor came across to chat to us and was obviously pleased to welcome us two international guests to his restaurant. In fact, to mark the occasion he insisted that all four of us should have an after-dinner drink 'on the house'. Then when we produced a camera he offered to take a picture of our group. This further example of American friendliness rounded off a very enjoyable day.

DAY 5

Today being Sunday, Maury and Mary were up quite early. They went to the first service of the day at the Roman Catholic church where they are members. By the time they returned home Mary and I had risen at a much more leisurely pace. We all chatted for a while after breakfast (more of that lovely potato bread) and then Maury drove us into Frederick to the Episcopal Church which we had passed the previous day.

From the outside All Saints appeared as just a long, tall building. But once inside the elegant Gothic architecture was quite imposing. Two stewards were standing at the doorway and when we introduced ourselves as visitors from England we received an enthusiastic welcome. Another example of the warmth of American people. It was a large church and there must have been more than 200 in the congregation on this morning. We didn't see the rector, the parish priest; he was not on duty at this service. He had three assistant priests and this service was conducted by two of them.

Mary and I had a special interest in the music of the service as both of us have had many years of singing in church choirs and in addition I am an organist. From where we sat I couldn't actually see the organ or the lady playing it. I knew it was a lady because from the parish literature I saw that the Music Director was a lady and so was her Assistant—by coincidence both named Carol. The service began with a processional hymn and as they came up the centre aisle what a sight greeted us. A choir of almost thirty and including some twenty youngsters. If only we could have a choir like that back home in our own church. I would like to have had a look at the organ if there had been a chance. It had a lovely rich tone and gave a solid powerful lead to this large number of people in church.

The service, Sung Eucharist, was very similar to our corresponding service in the Church of England and so we felt that we were on familiar territory. But I noticed something of an international flavour in the Intercessions. One prayer began, "We pray for our companion parish, Holy Trinity, Tokyo." And prayers for the priesthood included a prayer for Archbishop Rowan. After the service ended one of those two stewards came to speak to us again and said, "I'm afraid that we don't pray for the Queen and the Royal Family as you do." I replied,

"No, but we won't hold that against you because you do at least pray for the Archbishop of Canterbury."

Back home for lunch and then came another memorable part of our holiday. Maury and Mary have had nine children, now all adults, and at present, as I write this, they have no less than 21 grandchildren. Today Mary and I were to meet most of this great family circle. The nine have been five boys and four girls. The eldest girl, Kathie, lived in Texas which was too far away for her to travel, but never mind—Mary and I had already met her a couple of times previously when she had been visiting England. And the second eldest son, Chris, lived in Seattle which is away on the far side of America on the Pacific coast and so also too far away for him to be with us. But the other seven all came along and also most of their children. Maury and Mary have a large home but as they said, "Bringing up nine children, we needed it!"

It appears that they have these family get-togethers from time to time and the organisation is quite slick. Obviously there had been some collaboration beforehand. As they arrived all the daughters brought a contribution towards the food and the sons went out to the garden to organise the barbecue. We were all keeping a close watch on the weather because the rain, which had been promised over the past two days, had not yet arrived but the sky was becoming rather overcast. As things turned out the day remained dry for us and so the barbecue went ahead but the temperature had dropped several degrees since our first two or three days in the States.

It was fascinating to learn how all these brothers and sisters have taken up careers in separate directions. The eldest son is Rick and he and I greeted each other as fellow accountants. He has built a successful practice in downtown Frederick. We met his wife Chrisse and their children. Then there was John who is a lawyer. His wife Lucy works in the travel industry and so she was pleased to have an opportunity to talk to someone from England. Next came Kevin, who works in satellite communications, with his wife Laura and then the youngest son is Steve who is a policeman. American police, like their British counterparts, are split into different sections and Steve is known as a state trooper.

So according to my reckoning, if someone steals money from you, Rick will calculate how much has been taken, Steve will arrest the culprit and John will fight your case in court. Talk about keeping it in the family.

As Kathie was not with us the eldest daughter present was Barbara with her husband Marty and their children. I spent some time chatting with Marty. He had served in the U.S. navy and thus travelled extensively but his knowledge of England was confined to the area immediately around London. Actually we found this to be the case several times during our holiday. Personally I think it is a great pity that many American visitors come to London but miss so much else that England has to offer. York, Stratford-upon-Avon, Bath, the Lake District. And that's before you even set foot in Scotland. Sometimes it seems that the furthest these visitors venture from London is to Windsor Castle. As time passed Mary and I got into the habit of telling people that our hometown is a few miles out of London on the Thames estuary. That satisfied everyone because they knew where London is. They could identify with that. Privately we said to each other, "It's a good job we don't come from somewhere like Huddersfield or Exeter. Nobody would ever fathom out where they are."

The two youngest daughters are Jan and Megan whom we knew quite well by now. We had seen Jan several times already as she lived quite close by in Walkersville and Megan had been with us on the visit to Washington. But there's a little story about Megan which is worth recording. When she arrived there was the usual type of greeting. "How are you, Megan?" "I'm not feeling at all pleased." "Oh, why not?"

It seems that the previous day she had used a car park where you get a certain time free but you have to pay in advance for any further time you want. When she returned to the car—well, she didn't because the car wasn't there. It was only a matter of minutes beyond the free time to which she had been entitled but the car had been impounded and taken to some central depot. It cost her $200 to get it back. That's roughly £140 in our money. The $200 covered a penalty for parking without paying the fee, the cost of removing the car and a standard administrative charge. Our Megan was not a happy bunny.

This story gives us a comparison between British and American attitudes. In Britain we have laws, orders, rules, instructions. But when someone breaks the law it seems so often that nobody makes a complaint, or if they do then the police do not press charges, or if they do then magistrates and judges hand down trivial and laughable punishments. A modern development in Britain is the 'suspended sentence', an arrangement whereby lawbreakers found guilty are not punished at all. But it is so different in America. There it is intended that laws are to be obeyed and those who break laws know in advance that they *will* be punished. In American eyes there is no point in having a law or rule if it is not treated with respect. They regard us Brits as being much too soft. To them Megan was entitled to a specified free parking period and not a minute more. Tough maybe, but that's the law.

DAY 6

We awoke to the sound of rain beating on the bedroom window. Heavy rain. It had arrived at last and, having arrived, it stayed with us all day without a single let-up. On the following day Mary and I would be saying goodbye to this lovely part of the States and winging our way across to California on the far Pacific coast. It would mean an early start and so today we spent part of the morning doing some advance packing. Rather that than feel that a somewhat dismal morning was wasted.

But Maury is not a man to be deterred by a little matter like the weather. He announced, "We'll have an early lunch and then we'll go to visit Fort Frederick this afternoon." The fort is 40 miles west of Frederick and to reach it we had to travel through part of the mountains on the western edge of Maryland. The scenery was quite spectacular even on a filthy day. Since returning to England I have read that according to archaeologists these mountains consist of sedimentary rock formed 350 million years ago. As we neared the Fort Frederick State Park, we were fascinated to see a group of black geese wandering quite casually at the roadside. They took no notice of us. And something else which caught our eye were rows and rows of miniature trees—dozens of them.

The fort is two lines of military quarters built inside a high stone wall which is in the shape of a large square. I quote some extracts from a leaflet which I picked up in the Visitor Centre.

> *The stone fort was erected in 1756 to protect English settlers from the French and their Indian allies. It was unique as most other forts of the period were built of wood and earth. It saw service again during the American Revolution as a prison for German and British soldiers.*
>
> *During the Civil War Union troops spent time at the fort and fought a brief skirmish with Confederate raiders on Christmas Day 1861. The fort's stone wall and two barracks have now been restored to their 1756 appearance.*

There have been a few occasions over the years when we have been caught out by the fact that British museums close on Mondays. It is something of a family joke that Mary and I needed three attempts to get inside the Ashmolean Museum in Oxford. Today we arrived at Fort Frederick, saw an almost empty parking area and decided that the bad weather was keeping people away. The entrance to the Visitor Centre was open but inside we found just two or three staff who pointed out that today, Monday, the place was closed. Just like home, I thought. But they had reckoned without Maury pleading his case. Not only had we driven a long way, he told them, but here were two visitors from England who might never again have an opportunity to see this piece of American history.

Oh, all right. (Well done, Maury.) They ushered the four of us into a side room which was already set up as a small cinema and switched on a short film about the history of the fort. A private showing, no less. Once again Mary and I had that feeling of being treated like very special international guests. Then we had a look around the Visitor Centre where there was a comprehensive display of military uniforms over the centuries. Afterwards we all went across to the barracks and found just one man working on some machinery in total solitude. Apparently on the previous day there had been a special event—maybe a reconstruction of some battle—and he was getting everything back into shipshape order again. He seemed pleased to have somebody to talk to on this horrible day and invited us to come inside the barracks away from the rain.

He knew a great deal about the history of the fort and so in effect we got a private talk and demonstration. You see, it pays to go to places when they are closed. He told us that his name was Trent Corbeau and he had a degree in history. He had travelled extensively, working mainly on research projects but also doing any other odd jobs which produced a few dollars. When he realised that were from England he said he had worked at the Tower of London for two years helping to compile literature for tourists. (But here again it was a case of an American who knew virtually nothing of England apart from London.)

Had it been a nice day we might possibly have strolled around part of the National Park. But the rain was coming down relentlessly and so it was a day for getting into the car and heading back to Walkersville. Before we left, Maury took a few photographs. So did Mary but her camera decided to be a bit temperamental and the ones she took did not develop very well. So after we returned to England Maury sent us copies of his pictures as otherwise we would have had no visual record of that day.

Along the way we passed through a built-up area where I noticed a few things that are different from what we know in Britain. Firstly we passed a school and signs outside indicated that a reduced speed limit applied in the immediate vicinity. This is common practice in America. In Britain there has long been widespread concern about accidents immediately outside schools. We know about the American system but many British motorists are strongly opposed to any restriction on their driving and so no politician (with one eye on the ballot box) has had the courage to put forward a specific proposition.

We came to some road works and I saw that what we know in Britain as a ramp is announced in America as BUMP. A bit terse, maybe, but it certainly catches the attention and gets the message across. Road works also mean that some signs need to be temporarily changed. Maury explained that when this happens, a red flag is placed above the sign. This indicates to drivers that the sign is temporary or even, maybe, a new one. Either way it tells the motorist that something is different and care is needed.

When we passed a gas station (garage, to you) I commented that the prices were displayed per gallon. Maury and Mary were surprised when I said that in England we show prices in litres. Why is that when we buy the fuel in gallons? I don't know—it is a typical English inconsistency. The gauge in our car at home is marked in gallons and if I want five gallons I wouldn't dream of asking for 22.73045 litres. Yet the only way I have of knowing in advance exactly how much it is going to cost me, the only way I can check whether the cashier has charged me correctly, is to multiply the published price by that figure—22.73045. I have often heard it said that foreigners don't understand the English. I wonder if part of the explanation might be that we don't understand ourselves.

For our final evening in Maryland we just sat and chatted until quite late. This time it was about our families. After all, we had already put the world to rights. We had already solved all the problems of modern society. Now we could just relax on a comfortable settee with a box of cookies and a glass of wine. Ah, this is the life, this is real living.

DAY 7

Up early this morning in time to enjoy our final breakfast in Maryland after which we dealt with the last items of our packing. Then came the moment to say goodbye to Maury's Mary and we thanked her profusely for the great week we had enjoyed. At the beginning they had both said, "Our home is your home" and they had really meant it. We could not possibly have had a more enthusiastic welcome

Then Maury drove us into Washington, back to Dulles Airport again. The rain of the previous day had gone but the sky was still very overcast. There was no problem parking right outside the terminal building and after unloading our bags from the car we now had to say our farewells to him. He had worked tremendously hard during the week to give us a memorable time and must have driven a few hundred miles. He knew we were taking loads of photographs as each day passed (in the end we filled three large albums when we got back to Southend) and I said that in addition I intended to write the story of our holiday. He asked me to let him have a copy in due course.

Checking in at the airline desk was quite straightforward and as we were making what is called an internal flight across America there were no Customs formalities to bother with. A great deal of building work was going on there, scheduled to take a few years, because there is ongoing pressure for considerable expansion of this airport. We faced a challenge in trying to find our departure gate. We thought we were heading in the right direction until we came to a solid wall but then we spotted a plan of the building. We studied it for a few moments but it made us even more confused than when we started. So we went back to the beginning, tried all over again and got it right this time.

When it was almost time to board the aircraft there was an announcement. "We have a slight technical problem. We have just put a full load of fuel into the aircraft but the gauges on the flight deck are showing less than full. Please accept our apologies—we have engineers working on the problem now and it should be only a short delay." But it was a half hour or so before they called us all to go on board. So we took off roughly forty minutes behind our scheduled time.

The aircraft was smaller than the one in which we had crossed the Atlantic and we did not have individual TV monitors at each seat. But there were plenty of overhead ones and when we were a little way into the flight these were switched on. But several were not working properly and so the whole lot were switched off again. Another apology over the public address system. It would be put right as quickly as possible. Great, I thought. Trust us to get an aircraft where the in-flight entertainment doesn't work and the crew don't know how much petrol we've got!

As we headed westward the weather steadily improved and by the time we finished our midday meal—yes, chicken again—the clouds had disappeared and we were surrounded by bright sunshine and blue skies. It meant that we were able to see something of the land we were flying over. If you draw a line across a map from Washington to Los Angeles it will cross part of the Grand Canyon. We had looked forward to seeing that but unfortunately there was some bad weather just in that area and so we were following a flight path that took us further south. However, as a result we saw something unexpected. Looking down we spotted lots of circles. Rows and rows of them, stretching to the horizon. It was rather like looking at some floor covering on which the pattern was simply circles, all the same size. After a few moments I realised what they were. Our original flight path would have taken us over the extreme northern tip of Texas but now we were further south and travelling over more of that state. What we were now seeing was part of the Texan oilfields. We were looking down on endless rows of storage tanks and from this angle they simply looked like plain circles. Hundreds of them, maybe thousands, but we must remember that these oilfields supply a very large proportion of the fuel used throughout the States.

Because of our changed flight path we crossed the southern edge of California, almost on the border with Mexico, then a little way out over the Pacific before banking round and approaching Los Angeles from the sea. I must give the full title, Los Angeles International, because there are three airports in the L.A. area. This change to our flight schedule meant that as we made our final approach to the airport we descended rather steeply. As a result Mary experienced a severe pain in her ears. It made her slightly deaf for the rest of the day and it was about three more days before the pain had finally gone completely.

The combination of a late start plus a slightly longer journey meant that in spite of having made good time we were still about forty minutes late arriving. All these internal flights normally use terminal building 6 but by the time we got there all the bays were occupied and so our aircraft was directed to a bay in terminal 7. We dealt with all the formalities quite quickly and walked through to the public area where Elizabeth and Phil were waiting to meet us.

They told us they had arrived in plenty of time and had made their way to terminal 6. Keeping an eye on the indicator boards they knew that we were running a bit late but could see which gate we would be arriving at. Then the message was changed to a different gate number so they walked to that one. Then the whole message was changed again to show that in fact we would be coming in to terminal 7. It's a different building, about ten minutes' walk away, but off they went and eventually that's where we all met up.

The next matter to be dealt with was reclaiming our luggage. Elizabeth and Phil were sure that all internal flight baggage would be taken to terminal 6 even though our aircraft had not been directed there. So the four of us walked there and spent some time scouring all the carousels. No sign of our flight number on any of the boards. Finally we came to the conclusion that the luggage must be at terminal 7 after all. We went back there and yes, there it was. Thus Mary and I spent our first hour in California marching backwards and forwards between two buildings.

Southern California is so completely different from Maryland. Most obviously, of course, it is much hotter. After taking off from Washington in the mid-60s we had now landed at Los Angeles in the low 80s. Elizabeth and Phil live in the city of Moorpark and as Phil drove us there we were fascinated to see avenues of palm trees along many of the roads. Then when we got away from the built-up areas we noticed that there were very few hedges or fences—the open fields came right up to the roadside. We saw cacti and citrus trees and pumpkins, the most enormous pumpkins you could ever imagine.

Naturally we had known years ago that the word 'distance' has rather different meanings to a Yank and a Brit. Elizabeth had told us that they live 'a little way' outside L.A. But to them a little way means an hour or so drive. It's rather like saying that Southend is a little way from Ipswich or Cambridge. To reach Moorpark from the airport we travelled on the freeway. As L.A. is one of the biggest cities in America the volume of road traffic is horrendous and this particular freeway had no less than six lanes in each direction. I think that five lanes are fairly common across America but several freeways around L.A. have six and believe me, all six are needed.

During the journey Elizabeth said, "We haven't organised an evening meal yet because we didn't know what you would want. We don't know what you have had on the aircraft. So after we have taken your luggage home we'll go along to the supermarket." That suited me fine. We had now been in America for a week and so far hadn't seen any shops apart from that shopping mall in Frederick. I was looking forward to seeing some real everyday shops.

Within walking distance from our home in Southend we have a branch of Tesco, the leading supermarket chain in Britain. And this branch is one of their largest. So Mary and I thought we knew what a big supermarket looked like. But when we walked into Ralph's at Moorpark we were staggered. It was big enough to take our Tesco at least twice. I think that was the moment when we fully began to realise just how much bigger everything is in America compared with Britain. Apart from noticing the freeways and the volume of traffic we had not really grasped this comparison whilst we were in Maryland. But here in California the sheer size of everything was overwhelming wherever we looked. As soon as we walked into Ralph's we saw the greengrocery display and I could hardly believe my eyes. Never had I seen such huge carrots, broccoli, peppers and tomatoes. Even the smallest potatoes were what I would have called baking potatoes.

And incidentally, this was when we also started to be aware of the size of so many American people. Now that we can look back over the entire holiday we have reached the conclusion that a great many Americans eat far too much and get hardly any exercise. They virtually live in their cars. During the month we saw many, many people who were so fat that they were, frankly, grotesque. Are they unconcerned about it? One must assume that many of them are, as otherwise they would surely have tried to do something about it.

After the evening meal we were shown around the home. It seems standard that on the ground floor American homes are open-plan style. In colder areas this spreads the heating more evenly and in hotter climates like California it helps that part of the home to remain pleasantly cool. The master bedroom was at the back of the house and so Mary and I would be using the second bedroom which was actually above the front door. But as the house was at the far end of a cul-de-sac there was no passing traffic. In fact, during our four weeks there it proved to be a very quiet room.

DAY 8

This was the day on which Mary and I started to learn about California as a whole and about this area to the north-west of Los Angeles in particular. We only travelled a short distance today but visited three cities. If that sounds slightly contradictory I must explain how the Americans understand the word 'city'.

In Britain we talk about a hamlet, village, town or city. I'm not sure whether there are any official definitions of those names but each gives you a rough idea of what to expect by way of population numbers. In America, however, you only hear the words town or city. Their town seems to correspond to our British village and to them everything else is a city.

California is the third largest of the 50 states (the other two are Alaska and Texas). It is actually almost twice the size of Great Britain, has a Pacific coastline of just under 1,000 miles and a population of 33 million. It took me a few days to get used to the idea that there are more than 40 cities in California until I realised that they use the word rather more freely than we do. It doesn't necessarily mean a huge population. Elizabeth and Phil live in Moorpark and today we also visited Thousand Oaks and Simi Valley.

And even when you are in the middle of a city you might not realise it! You see, there is so much space in America, endless land, an infinite supply. They don't need to cram everything together as we do in Britain. So the roads are wide, the houses have substantial gardens, the shops are large and have extensive parking space. Everywhere has this atmosphere of room to stretch and breathe.

But there is one drawback to all this. It means that wherever you want to go you will invariably have a long journey. Americans think nothing of commuting fifty or sixty miles to work each day. There is no question of children walking to school—it's much too far. That's why you see all those yellow school buses everywhere. They are not a luxury for lazy children; they are essential. And when Elizabeth goes shopping her nearest supermarket is almost three miles away. Yet she lives in a city.

Since returning to England Mary has been telling people that her strongest impression of American lifestyle is their absolute total dependence on the car. Now we realise why. For any active, healthy person, life in America would be almost impossible without a car. The distances involved in everyday life are so vast. Obviously, there are some elderly or disabled people who do not have cars but they must miss out on life to a much greater extent than their British counterparts. It came as a big surprise to both of us to discover that public transport in America is pathetic, in many places almost non-existent. Everybody around the world has heard of the American railroads and the Greyhound buses. So where are they?

I soon learned the answer. It was back in the 1920's and 1930's that the production and popularity of motorcars flourished. Led by Ford, the car giants were contributing a fortune to government funds by way of taxes but they also offered huge donations to be spent on building and developing the nation's roads. They were getting the best of both worlds, weren't they? Building all the cars for Americans to drive and also, out of their profits, building the roads on which to drive them, thus creating demand for still more cars. Gradually over the years people who had hitherto travelled by public transport became independent—the train and bus companies saw their passenger figures plummet and had to call it a day. There was no need for any Doctor Beeching to close down the railways—the companies themselves decided to do so before they went bankrupt.

Thus the situation today is that across America public transport is a rarity. With very few exceptions train services only operate at rush hour times. Each city has a few buses which operate only within that city boundary. There are very, very few buses available to convey you from one city to another. So for the average family there is just one answer. The car. Is it any wonder, therefore, that America is the source of so much pollution in today's world? The accusation often levelled is that the U.S.A. will not make any real effort to reduce its pollution levels. Based on what I have seen during my holiday I am inclined to the view that they *cannot* reduce those levels. Gradual developments over the twentieth century produced a situation where Americans are now totally committed to the car. They have no realistic option. I have read a report which says that in the States there are now 210 million cars. Yes, 210 million!! And that's just the private vehicles. When thinking about pollution levels, we must add to that figure all the commercial vans, trucks and taxicabs and all the emergency vehicles. (All right, get down off your soapbox, Doug.)

Today and during our holiday we were shown some of the local supermarkets. Elizabeth needed to stock up. The previous evening we had been to Ralph's, which was her nearest, but today she showed us two others. Wal-Mart and Von's. Okay, a supermarket is a supermarket, but we had an interest in these two. Wal-Mart is one of the American leaders and has recently moved into Britain by taking over our Asda. I was interested to see how they do things and what we might expect in Britain in future. And Elizabeth mentioned that there is a link between Von's in America and Safeways in Britain. So here is another candidate for a takeover.

We noticed one way in which American supermarkets are different from our own. In America the checkout cashiers do not sit on stools or chairs. They work standing up. When you stop to think about it, in Britain everyone in the retail industry stands up to work whether in vast hypermarkets, famous department stores or little village shops. With one exception—supermarket cashiers. Why are they different? But just imagine the uproar if companies like Tesco or Sainsbury were to ask their checkout staff to work standing up.

A little later while the ladies were preparing lunch I had a look at the local daily newspaper—116 pages in all and only 25 cents. That's roughly 18 pence in our money. As days went by I observed that 116 pages were about an average size. I couldn't help thinking that back home in Southend our daily paper is only half that size yet the price is 35 pence.

When Elizabeth and Phil first went to America they lived in Thousand Oaks, a city which is a little way out of Los Angeles. Well, that's what they told us. A little way out. Now we could see that in fact it is about forty miles out. That's 'a little way' to Americans. Apparently this part of California is very popular—no doubt because of the glorious weather—and the various towns and cities are growing quite rapidly. All over the place we saw new housing estates being built. The three cities we saw today—Moorpark, Thousand Oaks and Simi Valley—all now have populations of about 100,000 but because each covers such a vast area there is no sense of feeling crowded. Indeed, sometimes I looked around at the seemingly open land and thought, "Am I really in a city? So where *are* all the thousands who live here, so I'm told?"

I like the sound of the name Thousand Oaks. I am told that when the first few homes were built by land developers in the 1920's they held a competition to decide the name and this was the winning entry. Now that the area has grown into a city I could see that the oak is the most plentiful tree there but has anyone ever counted them to check the accuracy of the name? Very unlikely, was the answer.

Throughout our four weeks in California the temperature was in the 70's or 80's and we only had twenty minutes' rain in all that time. Because the weather is so reliable they can plan outdoor events with complete confidence. We walked through one park where there was a permanent shelter with seats and tables constructed of concrete and wood. Does that sound cold to sit on? Actually they were quite cool in the hot climate (there were no sides to the shelter) and not in any way uncomfortable. And to one side there was a permanent barbecue. Does this all belong to the local authority, I asked. Do people pay to hire the facility? Oh no, I was told, it's here for anyone who wishes to just come along and use it. I was very impressed by how spotlessly clean it all was. Obviously the local residents valued this amenity and treated it with respect.

Also in that same park we saw tennis courts, a basketball pitch and a beach volleyball court. This prompted a discussion about the American love of sport. We were told that many parks have similar facilities and all are used quite extensively. Sport is high on the lifestyle agenda in the States. It starts when they are children. I have already written that American schools begin at 8 a.m., or some even at 7.30, and they have their midday break literally at midday. After that break there are very few lessons and so the academic part of school life ends soon after 2.0. Then during the afternoon they all take part in sports. In the U.S. academic development and physical development are seen as being equally important. With that approach, and with all the facilities provided everywhere, is it any wonder that Americans appear to have a head start in international sporting contests?

From Thousand Oaks we drove on to the nearby city of Simi Valley. Quite frankly, this is your upper crust territory. Millionaires Row if ever I saw it. We had noticed already that American houses all have double garages but here in Simi Valley we saw houses which each had two doubles. And the so-called bungalows looked big enough to be almost hotels. So it was no surprise to learn that this is one area where your great Hollywood moguls live. Many properties were 'gated'—that is, there were huge iron gates across the driveways as a security measure. When we passed a golf clubhouse we were told that international film star Sylvester Stallone had applied for membership and been refused because he was not considered to be of the desired social class.

On the edge of Simi Valley is a large lake and so the immediate vicinity is known as Westlake Village. There were a number of yachts moored but we were told that the residents regard it as 'their' lake and are rather cool towards visitors.

To round off this our first full day with them Elizabeth and Phil suggested that we all go out for an evening meal. I remember that meal because Mary felt a little unwell (that problem with her ears) and was unable to finish her meal. A pity, because she had ordered what looked a delicious pie. But in America they are always quite happy for customers to take home a box—that's what we in England call a doggy bag. More than once during our four weeks we asked for a box. So Mary did in fact finish that pie the following evening.

I forget exactly what I ordered but the dish included some vegetables. When it arrived I stared disbelievingly at the most gigantic broccoli I have ever seen. Only one piece, one head, but it filled at least half the plate. Needless to say I didn't manage to eat it all but I think I did justice to the rest of the meal. I'm sure that was the evening when it really came home to me that enormous meals are a regular feature of American life. No wonder so many Americans are outrageously overweight. I was to find myself faced with a few more such meals in the weeks ahead. So you may not be surprised to hear that when I returned to England and weighed myself I found I had gained a stone during that one holiday.

DAY 9

Phil had to go into his office today. The company was working on an important project and a tight deadline was drawing close. He had been able to delegate a lot of the management aspect but not quite all. So today it was necessary to go in and check on how everything was progressing.

By now we had accumulated a collection of picture postcards all written and ready to send to our relatives and friends back in England. So Elizabeth took us along to the local post office and the first surprise for us was to see an open counter. No glass screens or security grilles. As there happened to be no other customers we chatted to the clerks for a few minutes and they were amazed when we told them how our post office staff in Britain need protection. And we also met a very good idea which is gradually being copied in our own country. In America all postage stamps are sold on backing sheets. The idea is slowly gaining ground in Britain but often it is still necessary for us to moisten the reverse side. Not in the States—that system was abandoned long ago. All you need to do is peel the stamp off the sheet and press it onto the envelope. So easy and hygienic.

And there is another American idea that may catch on in Britain. Although it is not a legal requirement, it is standard practice in America that all letters should carry a return address in the top left-hand corner of the envelope. Elizabeth showed us some stick-on labels she had printed on her computer and offered to do some for us. By coincidence, since our return to England the British Royal Mail people have been grumbling about the large number of letters they cannot deliver because addresses are either incorrect or incomplete. They are saying that if there were a return address shown then they could at least send the letters back. Perhaps we'll catch up with America one day.

On the way back home Elizabeth stopped to buy some gas (petrol to you). Another surprise for us. She stopped at a pump, inserted her credit card in the appropriate slot, keyed in the amount of fuel she wanted, placed the pump nozzle in the car's tank and walked away. Next to the pumps was a supply of soapy water and wiper blades and while the petrol pump was issuing the required amount of fuel she cleaned the front windscreen. Then she replaced the nozzle in the pump and we drove away. At no point did she go anywhere near the little shop where a cashier was sitting. She would have needed to go in if she had been paying by cash, of course, but in the U.S.A. most people use credit cards for most purchases. In fact, if you offer to pay by cash some shopkeepers look at you as if you're a little bit odd. (Quaint English foreigners.)

Americans are puzzled by our British system of filling the petrol tank first and then going into the shop to pay. "Why does anyone in your country ever pay for fuel? When you have filled up, why don't you then just drive away?" We told them that some people do indeed try it but almost all garages have closed circuit TV. They note the numbers of the relevant cars, trace the owners and take the offenders to court. Amazing though it may seem to our Yankee cousins, the vast majority of British motorists are honest and pay what they owe with no hesitation. Then we went back at them with our own question. "What happens when you supply those materials for motorists to clean their windscreens? How much is stolen?" They seemed surprised that we asked such a question because surely, they felt, Americans are honest.

So already, this early in our holiday, I was building up a picture showing that the Yanks are equally as inconsistent as us. Look—they demonstrate their honesty by not locking their cars. Remember how Maury left his unlocked for the best part of three hours at Gettysburg? They trust people not to steal windscreen washing equipment and they have no protective screens in their post offices. Yet, by contrast, they won't let you have a single drop of fuel until you have paid in full in advance. No, I have come to the conclusion that the Yanks are lovely people and they are just as inconsistent as we are! (And something else I encountered later. When you use a credit card they sometimes ask to see full supporting evidence, including a photograph, as proof that you indeed are whom you claim to be. In all the years that I have used a credit card in Britain I have never once been asked to produce a supporting photo.)

We were surprised at something else which Elizabeth did on the way home. Remember that they drive on the opposite side of the road to us. We stopped at traffic lights—we were going to turn right and so were in the inside lane. While the lights were still red she calmly drove round the corner. Seeing our reaction she explained that as no other vehicles were approaching from the left she could make that turn, against the lights, because she was not crossing any other traffic. Obviously if other cars had been approaching she would have had to wait until they passed, but as soon as the way was clear she no longer needed to wait for the lights to change.

"We can see the logic," we said. "It obviously speeds up the traffic. It's a useful option to have."

"Oh, it's not just an option," she replied. "It's something which is expected automatically. In fact, if you don't do it the drivers behind all get very uptight."

Here again, since our return to England, one of our government transport spokesmen has suggested that the corresponding idea could be introduced here—turning left against a red light—but it doesn't appear to have received a very enthusiastic welcome.

Armed with her Bachelor of Music honours degree from Manchester University, Elizabeth is a qualified music teacher and back home before lunch she gave a violin lesson to a lady named Sharon. The two of them were members of the Moorpark Symphony Orchestra. Sharon was not a regular pupil of Elizabeth's but there was a big concert coming up and Sharon was having a few problems with the second violin line. So Elizabeth was giving her some help. Although Mary and I kept well out of the way, we could hear the entire practice because of the open plan nature of the house. Afterwards we had a short chat with Sharon who was feeling very excited (and nervous) about the concert.

Another member of the orchestra, hearing of our 'maiden visit' to America, had told Elizabeth that we might enjoy a visit to the Stagecoach Inn Museum. So as it was only a short distance away, we went there straight after lunch. It's actually a complex, which, in addition to the main museum building, includes some stagecoaches, an early Model A Ford, a windmill, a blacksmith's shop and masses of pictures and artefacts covering the history of this immediate part of California. As it was a midweek afternoon there were not many customers and we spent quite a while chatting to the guides on duty. (In America they are called docents—pronounced doe-sense.)

One point amused me, but in order to remain discreet I kept it to myself. These local folks spoke of the museum with great awe, almost reverence, telling us it dates back to 1876. It was, they said, originally the Grand Union Hotel back in the era when the stagecoach was a universal form of transport. But hold on—a few minutes later they were telling us that it was threatened with demolition in the mid-1960's. New roads were being built and so in order to preserve the museum it was painstakingly moved a few miles to its present site. Then in 1970 it was completely devastated by a fire of 'undetermined origin' along with most of the contents. So what we see today is a full-size replica building constructed in the period from 1976 to 1980. I admire the effort and devotion that went into all this reconstruction and the attention to exact detail. But I couldn't help smiling to myself when I heard them talking about the building as if it were the actual original.

We left the Museum in time to make the twenty minutes' drive to Phil's office and arrive there shortly before everyone would be going home. We had been hearing a lot about a chap named Umrao, a 100% American with an Indian ancestry. Elizabeth particularly wanted us to meet him.

When Phil had made the big decision to move to America in 1997, he had taken up a management post in a company making computer games. This is a market that is nowadays expanding at a breathtaking rate. Five years later an entrepreneur named Umrao set up his own company in that same line of business and Phil went with him as Technical Director. This made him joint number two along with the Artistic Director. The venture has been so successful that it is no secret that Umrao is now a millionaire. And Phil quietly admits that he himself has picked up a few dollars along the way.

The company's offices are on the second floor of an attractive Moorish-style building and so we stepped into an elevator and pressed button number 3. You see, in America they never use the term 'ground floor'. In their language that's floor number 1 and so what we call the first floor is to them floor number 2, and so on. Of course, offices are by their very nature not exactly tourist attractions, but we found one unusual feature here. Apparently the receptionist had gone home unwell and as nobody else was immediately available the Artistic Director, no less, was manning the counter, dealing with the evening's outgoing post and operating the switchboard. There's socialism for you. And everyone was keeping him so busy he hardly had a moment to shake hands with us.

The staff, numbering around thirty, were working in a network of rooms opening off two central corridors. We were escorted along to one larger office and there Umrao greeted us warmly. I am not particularly good at estimating ages but would place him as around forty. He had lived his entire life in California and was yet another Yank whose knowledge of England consisted of just London. We must have been talking for about half an hour—Umrao himself, Elizabeth and Phil, Mary and me. He was a very natural and relaxed man with a keen sense of humour. What's more, he was thoroughly unassuming and modest. Was I really chatting with a millionaire?

When it was time to leave he stood at the door to see us on our way. I was last in the line and after saying goodbye to me he paused. Still holding my hand he nodded in the direction of Phil and said very quietly, "He's the smartest guy on the team." To me this was an example of something I have frequently heard about over the years. Americans are quite proud of their education system but they also have a tremendous respect for our British standards. In the States anyone with a British education, especially at university level, has got a head start. It was obvious to me that Umrao was delighted to have Phil as his right-hand man.

DAY 10

This morning Elizabeth was doing various jobs around the house and Phil had to go to a business meeting. So Mary and I did something that is just about as un-American as is humanly possible. We went for a walk. Yes, we actually walked—in America!

They don't do that sort of thing. Obviously this business of distance that I have already mentioned is an important factor, but in my opinion even when they could walk, they don't. When they step outside their homes the natural instinct is to open the car door and get in. I frequently found myself wondering why they build pavements in America. They hardly ever get used. Why not use that space to put in another lane of traffic?

By now we were getting used to the temperature in California. Even in the mid-80's it did not seem excessively hot and so a quiet stroll in the morning was quite enjoyable. We took the opportunity to see something of the district immediately around our holiday home. We actually walked for almost an hour and a half and in all that time the only other pedestrian we met was a man exercising his dog. And don't forget that we were on the outskirts of a city with almost 100,000 residents!

We passed a school and were impressed by the facilities provided in the school fields. It is such a strange contrast that Americans attach great emphasis to the physical development of their children, yet, at the same time, everyone eats enormous meals. Quite a lot of American women, for example, make the Vicar of Dibley look anorexic. And it's not just the adults. In spite of all this athletic activity there are, as I write, five million American children who are obese. Five million!! And that's in an official report. They're not just fat—they are obese, with all that this implies for their future.

The situation was explained to me. Very few American children go home at lunchtime, again because of the distance. So the school canteens do a roaring trade. The cost to the schools is covered partly from public funds and partly by parents. But then along come the fast food giants—McDonalds, Burger King, and so on. They tell the schools, "If you promote our products in your canteens we will pay you a handsome commission." So it is not surprising that the schools take the money. The schools win because they then have an additional source of revenue that they can use on improving school facilities. The companies win because from an early age they have future customers, converts to the fast food culture. The only people who lose are the children themselves who grow steadily fatter and fatter. But when there's money up for grabs, does anyone really care about children? Up until now it would seem not, but at last the first mutterings of concern are being heard. People are also starting to question the amount of food advertising in magazines and on TV, which is specifically targeted at children. It will be interesting to see which way the pendulum swings in future—health or profit.

We also passed a Mormon church and it prompted us to think about the different churches we were seeing in the States. The one we had attended in Frederick had apparently been the only Episcopal church in the city. Roman Catholic churches are also a bit thin on the ground. Whilst in Maryland we had noticed a large number of Lutheran churches and that, I suppose, reflects the German and Dutch origins of that area. Here in California the Mormons are quite numerous and so also are the Seventh Day Adventists. But right across America we noticed that a great many Christians seem to refer to themselves as The Church Of Jesus Christ. We wondered just what that implies. Is there any kind of link between the churches, any kind of co-operation, or is each one a separate and isolated group? From the newspaper notices we saw that there is never any use of titles such as Priest or Pastor. The leader of each church is known simply as the Preacher. I have referred previously to the great American emphasis on personal freedom in all walks of life. Possibly this could be another example—people feeling that "I want to worship God in my own way without any formalities or organisations being involved".

We had to smile as we turned into the road where Elizabeth and Phil live. A notice at the roadside warns that road-sweeping is carried out every Thursday and that vehicles left causing an obstruction will be towed away. Believe you me, they mean it. No messing about. Do you recall that incident a week or so earlier when Megan's car was towed away? All she had done was leave it parked for a few minutes beyond the free time she had been entitled to. Back home in England we get our road swept about once a month, at no set time, and as they come along they simply swerve around all the cars left at the kerbside. But not in the States. In that country they mean what they say. You are given fair warning, you know the rules and if you deliberately ignore them, then the car *will* be towed away.

Elizabeth had prepared sandwiches and Mary and I would have been willing to eat them in the garden. But Elizabeth told us it was not a very good idea in such a climate. We were already aware that there was a fine mesh over the patio door in order to keep out flying insects. (It's called a bug screen.) While you are out in the open air you are not conscious of them, but no doubt you soon would be if you produced some attractive food. So it was lunch indoors.

We did a bit more local shopping in the afternoon. 'Local' means we didn't go further than about ten miles! As we drove along we saw something which is apparently quite commonplace in the States—a car supermarket. For about a mile alongside the road there were hundreds and hundreds of cars, new and second-hand, every conceivable make and model and all ages. When buying a car there is no need to trail around loads of showrooms trying to remember what you saw two days ago. Here there is ample choice and variety and you can compare prices on the spot. An excellent idea, but another example of what can be done when there is sufficient space. I am told that there are people wanting to introduce this to Britain but, of course, the problem is finding enough room.

We didn't stay out too long because Elizabeth and Mary were going out in the evening. Well, in the late afternoon, actually. Two of the great loves of Elizabeth's life have been music and the Girl Guide movement. (In America they are called Girl Scouts.) She has been able to use these to help her settle into a new country and get to know people. As a result she is nowadays involved in training sessions and this evening was to be one of those. Mary has been a member of the Guide movement almost all her life—that's obviously where Elizabeth gets it from—and she had been invited to go along as well. It meant a fairly long drive and so they both set off before Phil was home from the office. As a result I was on my own for a short time but I took the opportunity to renew an acquaintance with a piano. You see, some years previously a family friend of ours had given her piano to Elizabeth and we had organised its transfer from Southend up to North Yorkshire. I had played it once or twice while it was still in Southend and also while it was up there in Yorkshire. Then, when Elizabeth and Phil moved from England to California, they shipped all their furniture across. I hadn't seen the piano for just over seven years but now, some five and a half thousand miles from where we had last met, I had the chance to play it again. So I did, for about half an hour until Phil arrived home. Thoroughly enjoyed myself.

I saw a double-decker train that evening. What happened was that Phil and I decided to have a Chinese takeaway so he phoned the order through and then we went to collect it. On the way we saw this train. Like you, I am quite familiar with double-decker buses and luxury coaches. But a train? I had to look twice. I have already written about the lack of public transport in America and when I told Mary later about this train I said I hoped she would see one for herself. But in fact we didn't see another train for the whole of our holiday—not one. That's how scarce they are.

This brings us to the first of just two occasions in our holiday when Mary and I were not together. So I'll pass the baton to her and she will tell you about her evening with some Girl Scout leaders and Brownies.

◆ ◆ ◆

The journey took us an hour or so along the freeway away from Los Angeles. It was a new part of California to me but I noticed that we passed Ventura, a town which Elizabeth had on her list for us to visit. Finally we turned off the main road and drove up into the mountains. Our destination was the Arnaz Programme Centre, a campsite and training ground owned by the Girl Scouts Association. There is a reception building and also a Pack Holiday hut for Brownies.

The occasion was a training weekend for Girl Scout leaders. They all arrived in time to prepare their evening meal that was an exercise in foil cooking. Elizabeth and I had taken with us what we considered to be reasonable size meals but I was amazed at what huge portions some of the leaders were cooking.

Their approach to leadership in the States is not the same as ours in Britain. When their daughters join the movement the mothers are expected to become involved in leading the unit. But the result is that when a girl moves up from Brownies to Girl Scouts, the mother moves with her. As soon as the girl leaves Girl Scouts the parents leave too. This produces a continual changeover of leaders. I felt, and Elizabeth agrees with me, that parents' interest was directed solely to the unit and not to the movement as a whole.

But I must say straight away that they all made me very welcome and were keen to ask me all about Guiding in Britain. They knew that I am President of my local District but I'm sure they were very surprised when I said I had previously been District Secretary for thirteen years and had run a Brownie Pack for twenty years. What, a Pack which didn't involve my own daughter? To my mind this perpetual change of leaders prevents any continuity developing. It is certainly true that their leaders in America have very little knowledge of the worldwide movement and its history.

A couple of fathers were there as well and during the evening one of them gave a talk on various aspects of woodcraft. Then after we had eaten our meal it was time for the campfire and twelve Brownies who were staying in the Pack Holiday hut came across to join us. This was Elizabeth's part of the evening. Singing around the campfire seems to be a new idea to Americans. Elizabeth's musical knowledge and experience means that she is now accepted in that area as an authority, a trainer, on this particular activity. This evening she taught the leaders a few songs which she had brought with her from England.

In due course it was bedtime for the Brownies and after I had taken one or two photographs we also made a move for home. Elizabeth said that had she been there on her own she would have stayed the night and gone home the following morning. But our visit to the U.S.A. was the first time she had seen us for a couple of years and she wanted to spend the time with us. So it was a long drive back in the dark.

DAY 11

This morning we had a quiet few hours at home. I took the opportunity to read the local newspaper and I needed a morning because it wasn't the usual 116 pages. As this was a Saturday the paper, today was 144 pages! But still the same price, still only 25 cents. Being the weekend there were a number of leaflets enclosed and I am told that these money-off coupons are even more of a feature in the States than they are in Britain. Elizabeth and Phil put to one side any coupons which they feel they may use in due course and I saw that they do indeed have quite a large collection. I was also observing when we were in the supermarkets that customers were handing over their coupons by the armful.

We watched TV for a while. I have already mentioned that the Olympic Games were in progress and everyone was excited at the TV stations because the American athletes were doing so well. I was having great difficulty trying to find out how the Brits were getting on. Of course, I wouldn't dream of suggesting that all the American commentators were biased (just because their lot were winning almost as many medals as everyone else added together). Arr-sm it was, arr-sm.

Mind you, I reckon we were lucky to see any programmes at all on TV. Back home we grumble about all the interruptions from advertisements, but those are not a patch on what they get on American TV. It seems that every few minutes there is a break in the programme and then come yet more endless adverts. I suppose it's something you can get used to after a few years but I certainly found it irritating. And all their stations are commercially sponsored so there's no escape. They don't have anything that is equivalent to our B.B.C.

On the subject of TV, I learned something that pleased me, something in which the British are ahead of the Yanks. In Britain we can watch one TV station and at the same time record a programme on another station. Mary and I frequently do this when two programmes are shown at the same time and we want to see both. But they can't do that in America. They can record any programme whilst the set is turned off or they can record the programme which they are actually watching. But they don't have the option which we in Britain take for granted. One up to us.

The garden needed some attention and so after lunch we went to the local garden centre. Even this was so much larger than any we had seen in England. Theirs sell the same types of products as ours but in such big quantities—enormous piles of decorative pavings, hundreds of bags of compost. Never have I seen so much timber fencing. What Phil was after was something to get rid of gophers. We learned that a gopher is a type of mole. He had noticed that some telltale little mounds of earth were appearing around his lawn. It seems that the accepted way of dealing with them is to bore small holes in the grass and place pellets under the surface. He hadn't actually tried this yet and so didn't know how effective the idea was. But it was worth a try. Back home he spent the next hour or so trying to deduce exactly where the tunnelling was happening and setting the bait. But I suppose you cannot tell whether you have succeeded or not until the mounds no longer multiply.

While we were all out there in the garden we met the next-door neighbours, an Asiatic family. Lovely people, tremendously friendly, and with a large dog which bounded around making a great fuss of everybody. Asiatic? Yes, I must explain that in this part of the U.S. the population is extremely mixed. Mexicans, Spanish, British, Japanese, Malayans, Canadians. (Oh, and some Americans.) But apparently they are not referred to by their separate nationalities. You will hear the words Hispanic or Asiatic used. In fact, I was told at one point that the Japanese residents in America get a little bit uptight if they are not called Asiatic.

Mary and I congratulated the neighbours on the colourful flag outside their house. Since our arrival in the States we had noticed flags everywhere—usually, but not always, the Stars and Stripes. At first we had put this patriotism down to the success in the Olympics, but now we were told this is not so. We learned that in America it is almost standard practice to have a flagpole outside each house. I already knew that in schools they start each day by singing The Star-Spangled Banner whilst facing the flag, but this business of flags outside the home was news to me. They are used as a form of decoration and certainly brighten up the neighbourhood. There was the Great Bear, which is the Californian state flag, there were flags showing children's story characters, and we saw a number relating to the forthcoming Hallowe'en weekend

And I'll tell you something else about American homes that puzzles me—their system of numbering. In Walkersville Maury and Mary live at the first house in a road which seems only about two hundred yards long. Yet their house number is 8797. In Moorpark Elizabeth and Phil live in a cul-de-sac where there are only nine houses. Yet their number is 15288. I asked how these numbers are worked out but never really got a straight answer. I think that maybe it is something similar, but certainly not identical, to our British national grid numbers. There was some suggestion that the emergency services are involved somewhere along the line, that if you quote a house number then somebody else can refer to a map and immediately identify the exact location of any building. But it seemed that nobody could tell me categorically that this was the answer. In short, nobody actually knew. And I noticed while talking to those neighbours that their house was numbered 15272 and the house beyond them was 15280. So the numbers didn't even run in sequence.

On reflection I think I prefer our British system of starting at one end of the road with the number 1 and then moving upwards from there. My little brain can cope with that.

Those house numbers are also painted on the kerbside outside each property and on the day when the dustmen come the residents place all their wheelie bins next to their number at the kerbside. And incidentally, refuse collection is not included as part of the local authority's duties. It is done by private contractors and the householders have to pay for the service. But one aspect of American life is the same as ours in Britain. The level of enthusiasm for recycling seems to vary from one district to another. Some authorities take it quite seriously whilst others apparently couldn't care less. Just like England, isn't it?

Oh, by the way—something else I learned today. 'Noughts and crosses' is a popular game in America but they have their own name for it. They call it Tick-Tack-Toe. You really needed to know that, didn't you?

DAY 12

With our breakfast this morning we tried some corn bread. Quite tasty, though had I not known the name I would have said it was Madeira cake. I also noticed something unexpected. In Britain the Weetabix Company proudly display the Royal warrant on their packaging. Quite right, too—good luck to them. But somehow I hadn't quite expected to see it on the packets they sell in America. Deep down inside I felt a little tingle of pride at seeing our Royal coat of arms in this 'foreign strand'. And then those two magic words, 'By Appointment'. Should I have stood to attention while I typed that?

As the fall (that's the American word for autumn) moves into early winter, there is a veritable spate of festive occasions. They celebrate Labour Day, Veterans Day, Columbus Day, Hallowe'en and then Thanksgiving Day. All these within the space of September—October—November. What they don't celebrate is the Harvest Festival, which is so familiar to us in Britain. But their Hallowe'en is a kind of combination of Harvest plus public holiday plus carnival. The pumpkin plays a very prominent part in the celebrations and we had seen several advertisements for pumpkin fairs.

This weekend an announcement in the local newspaper caught our attention. The Tierra Rejada Family Farm was open to visitors and as it was only a short distance away we decided to go and see what it was like. And what an absolute gem it turned out to be! The farm consisted of several huge fields and three of these were open to visitors, one of them set aside as a car park. The second one was full of pumpkins—hundreds and hundreds of them—all sizes, as far as the eye could see—I'm not kidding. Every one was for sale and many were far too big and heavy to be carried. At the gateway a farm worker sat at a table taking the money and next to him was a row of wheelbarrows. People were taking a barrow, heaving a great big pumpkin onto it, wheeling it to their car and then bringing the barrow back. Meanwhile a Clydesdale horse-drawn wagon was taking children for rides around the field and there were also some pony rides. We had never seen anything like it. Some of the pumpkins were no bigger than melons whereas others were so enormous that it needed two people to lift them.

There were hundreds of people there but once again because of the endless space in America it didn't seem at all crowded. And the third field was wonderful. Here there were stallholders selling all manner of craft items and others selling a great assortment of fresh fruit and local vegetables. Under a gazebo (for even in mid-morning it was already pretty hot out there in the middle of the field) was a small band playing genuine Country and Western music. The farm staff had built a haystack mountain that children could climb and there were various sideshows with games and face painting. Layers of straw had been put down everywhere, making a soft carpet for people to walk on.

We felt almost bowled over by the wonderful atmosphere and I think Mary's delighted exclamation summed it all up: "Oh, it's just like a scene out of Oklahoma!" On this beautiful sunny morning everyone was having a great time and Phil remarked, "Now you can say that you've been to the real true America. This is something that the tourists never get to see." We did in fact buy two packets of home-made biscuits with the intention of taking them back to England but that idea fell by the wayside because two days later we had eaten them! They were absolutely gorgeous, the kind that just melt in your mouth. Sorry, you'll just have to take my word for it.

Elizabeth and Phil had bought a few things as well and so it was back home for lunch before setting off on our second excursion of the day. This was to the Chumash Interpretative Centre at Oakbrook Regional Park. That's an almighty mouthful, isn't it? Chumash is pronounced shoe-marsh and this was the Indian tribe who had originally settled in what later became southern California. More about that later, but for now let me quote a few sentences from a leaflet I picked up during this afternoon's visit.

> The Chumash people have lived for centuries along the Californian coast and inland areas. Spanish missionisation followed by Mexican and then European American occupations meant destruction of the Chumash way of life. Much of this is now being rediscovered, recorded and preserved.
>
> Archaeologists have found evidence of early hunting settlements as far back as 35,000 years ago. Their first contact with any Europeans was when the Spanish explorer Juan Cabrillo arrived in the Santa Barbara Channel in 1542. One tragic result was the arrival of European diseases such as measles and smallpox.
>
> When gold was discovered in northern California thousands of Americans arrived and then came even more after California became a state. Laws at that time did not protect Indians and they could be forced off their lands.
>
> An estimated 1,500 still live in the area today.

Off we went, then, to this Oakbrook Park. It was well off the beaten track and at first appeared to be some kind of sprawling wilderness at the foot of the Santa Monica Mountains. But as we drew near we found a small modern building which houses a museum. In this there are numerous artefacts, maps, drawings and descriptions of the Chumash life in those far-off days. At the reception desk were two Indians. From a distance you could tell they were Indians because of their hairstyle and the colour of their skins. But a blind person would not have known because when they spoke they sounded like any other American. It seemed somewhat incongruous to see Indians dressing and talking just like ordinary Yanks and brought home to me just how much this ethnic minority has integrated into today's culture.

From this building, after spending some time looking around the exhibits, we then went outside to the grounds which were just as a typical reservation would have been all those centuries ago. Immediately it was as if we were miles from anywhere. We followed a dust trail until in due course—after stopping to study and photograph a big lizard that showed no interest in us whatsoever—we came to a large clearing. This was the centre of a typical Chumash village. To one side there were full-size reproductions showing stage by stage how the mud hut type of dwelling had been constructed. We could see the basic skeleton and then how various skins were overlaid and then the tightly-packed earth to give the finished home. There were also rows of permanent benches set out in this clearing and apparently it is the scene of various ceremonies and festivities illustrating the Chumash life. Unfortunately nothing like that was happening while we were there.

We strolled back along the trail to the building where Elizabeth made a few enquiries about guided tours for youngsters. She had in mind bringing the Girl Scouts along one day. I think she was able to get a couple of useful leaflets and we then made our way back to the car. In a sense we felt a little sad. We had had a brief insight into a people and a way of life which has now been almost lost. Lost in the sense of being swept aside by the mad rush of these past few centuries. These Indians appeared, and indeed still do appear, to be a calm, gentle people concerned only with living their own lives. In their hearts they may feel bitter about how the world has treated them but even now they don't show it. Rather are they proud of their heritage and keen to show it and explain it to our modern frenetic so-called 'civilisation'. On this quiet sunny afternoon there was hardly any breeze, hardly any sound of birds as we walked along these thickly wooded paths. In such an atmosphere it was easy to understand how these Indians always appeared to be at peace with the world. Even we products of the twentieth century could relax and just let the natural world take control of us for a short time.

> What is this life if, full of care,
> We have no time to stand and stare—
> No time to stand beneath the boughs
> And stare as long as sheep or cows?

We returned home, motoring back into our everyday world. For Mary and me one purpose of this journey to the States had been to learn about life in this the leading nation of the western world. In so doing we were learning about what the twentieth century has achieved. But this afternoon, for just two or three hours, we had been reminded also of what the twentieth century has lost. I think this little experience had done me good.

I have just called America the leading nation of the western world. But they ain't out front on everything. This evening I discovered an example of how Britain is ahead of them so it gave our patriotic ego a nice boost. It concerned telesales calls. Americans are becoming increasingly annoyed because they are getting more and more sales calls at home. Is there anything they can do to stop it? Ah, they have come up with an idea for subscribers to put their names on a list of private residents who do not wish to receive such calls. But wait a minute. We have been doing this in Britain for a long time. We call it the Telephone Preference Service and subscribers can register with it free of charge. Mary and I did so a few years ago. Previously we had sometimes been getting two or three calls a day but since we registered we have been receiving no more than three in a whole year. Come on America, wake up! Get with it.

Elizabeth and Phil have sufficient space in their home for a pool table and so after dinner this evening Phil introduced me to the mysteries of American pool. I am conversant with the rules of snooker and billiards but only have a vague idea about British pool. So it wasn't too difficult for me to tackle a new version. The most important lesson I learned was that the Americans don't allow fluke shots. At one point I was aiming to pot a ball in a centre pocket but slightly mis-hit the cue ball. The target ball, instead of going into the pocket, cannoned onto another ball which rolled along the cushion into a corner pocket. I'm told that you can't count that score in America. Before making the shot you have to declare what you are aiming to pot.

I enjoyed the session but (*sshh*—whisper this very quietly) I still think that snooker requires more skill.

DAY 13

During our four weeks in California we went to several places that have an historical significance. Today's visit to Santa Barbara was a fine example. So I think now is the moment to include a very brief thumbnail history of this part of the world.

More than 10,000 years ago nomadic tribes from Asia crossed the Bering Straits from Siberia to Alaska and gradually spread through what is now Canada, the U.S.A. and South America. I'm sure everyone knows that when Christopher Columbus landed in 1492 he thought he had arrived in India. As the native people had a coppery coloured skin they became known as Red Indians. Those who settled in what is now California were the Chumash tribes.

In the early years of the 16th century Spanish explorers came to this part of North America but it was another 200 years before Franciscan missionaries arrived to teach Christianity. Along the coastal areas they established a chain of missions and many of these still exist in various stages of preservation. A mission consisted of a Roman Catholic church with living accommodation for the priests plus facilities for teaching the local people, caring for the sick and providing hospitality to travellers.

Then in the first half of the 19th century it all happened:

    1811   Mexico declared its independence from Spain.
    1812   California withdrew its allegiance from Spain and joined Mexico.
    1813   California was officially declared American.
    1814   The discovery of gold in California caused the famous 'gold rush'. California joined the United States.

After the heady days of the gold rush some terribly hard times followed. Wages fell to a very low level; there was widespread poverty and unemployment. Yet many Mexicans stayed because even these harsh conditions were better than those back home in Mexico. Actually, the situation still exists today whereby California has an illegal immigrant problem much the same as our problem in

England. Mexicans frequently prefer to live in California, accepting menial jobs and poor living standards rather than return to their native country.

In the 20th century the film industry blossomed and made its home at Hollywood, a district of Los Angeles. That location was chosen because the weather there is pretty reliable throughout the year and within easy reach of L.A. is every type of background scenery—large modern cities, small Western-style townships, ocean, bleak desert, snow-capped mountains, you name it. It is this film industry that has given southern California its modern aura of glitz and glamour.

Okay—end of history lesson.

Today we motored towards the coast to join the P.C.H. That's the Pacific Coast Highway, one of America's best-known roads. It stretches along the Californian coast from Santa Monica to San Francisco and is picturesque, even breathtaking, because all the way there is this great combination of ocean on one side and mountain scenery on the other. Our destination today was Santa Barbara, a city with almost 100,000 residents about forty miles north of Moorpark.

At times it wasn't the most luxurious of journeys because great many American freeways are constructed with a ribbed concrete surface. Only the local roads have tarmac. Obviously it's a safety feature, but I don't know whether the motive is related to extreme weather conditions or to speeding drivers. It is not terribly uncomfortable but at the same time it certainly doesn't give the smooth ride of a tarmac surface. And something else surprised me. Phil took a call from his office on his mobile. We told him afterwards that this has now been made illegal in Britain and he said that although it has been discussed in the States nobody has had the courage to try and change the law. I suppose it's yet another example of Americans jealously guarding their right to Freedom—freedom to do what they want when they want.

Oh, talking of American roads, an amusing little story which Elizabeth told us. When she took up residence in the States she held a British driving licence. They will accept that for temporary visitors, but not on a permanent basis. So she had to take one of their driving tests. As she got into the car the examiner said, "First, I want to watch your driving from outside the auto so I'll go and stand at that corner. Just drive down the pavement towards me." Drive down the pavement? Fortunately she suddenly remembered that in their language the pavement is the tarmac surface on the road. What we call the pavement is to them the sidewalk. After that little moment she passed the test first time.

The seaside city of Santa Barbara has over the years become established as an upmarket area. It is a very attractive city to look at, being at a point where the coast sweeps gently round forming a large bay. So as you approach it from the south you have the Santa Ynez Mountains on your right and the Pacific Ocean on your left. You are greeted by a beautiful vista of white stucco walls and red tiled roofs. There is a strong Spanish-Moorish atmosphere everywhere, a genteel sophistication that is quite relaxing.

On arriving there we drove through the city to the Mission. This was founded in 1786, is the best preserved of the 21 Californian missions, and is popularly known as the Queen of the Missions. A party of schoolchildren were being escorted around the complex, but apart from them there were only a handful of other visitors. The complex still functions as a Franciscan friary as well as a parish church and museum. Over the main door are three sets of skulls and crossbones. But a close inspection reveals that only one set is carved in stone—the other two sets are real bones! The church itself is big enough to hold several hundred worshippers and is filled with Chumash wall decorations and art from the 18th and 19th centuries. I spent some time admiring the grandeur and opulence of the high altar and large sanctuary. But this was in striking contrast to the tiny stark bare rooms beyond the church that provided 'living accommodation' and space for private prayer and study.

After leaving the Mission we headed back downtown in search of lunch. 'Downtown' is the word Americans use to describe the centre of any town or city. We had noticed posters advertising bus tours of the city, but closer scrutiny revealed that they don't operate on Mondays. That Monday business again, you notice. So instead, we took a leisurely stroll along the short pier where further posters mentioned boat trips for whale watching. What a pity we didn't have time for one of those. Something to bear in mind for the future. Then back on shore we made our way to Main Street. In Britain the principal shopping area of a town is usually called High Street or High Road—in the States it's always Main Street.

As we meandered along, window-shopping in the afternoon sunshine, I saw something that horrified me. Three men who looked decidedly scruffy were gathered around a kerbside rubbish bin. They were emptying out the contents on the pavement, scrabbling for scraps of food and greedily eating anything they found. It's easy to read about such people or to watch TV programmes, but the situation smacks you on the nose when you meet it in real life. Even now, some time later, I still find it difficult to describe my feelings that afternoon—a confused jumble of disbelief, disgust and amazement. These were grown men, not little children who, it might be argued, did not know any better. The spectacle would have been bad enough after dark when not too many people might see it. But no, this was a busy street in broad daylight. These three men had fallen to a level where they had absolutely no self-respect. They had lost every last tiny vestige of human dignity; they were akin to alley cats. I'm not ashamed to admit that the incident shook me for a few minutes.

And looking back on it now, some time later, another aspect occurs to me. While this was going on dozens of Americans were passing to and fro. Nobody batted an eyelid. Nobody seemed the slightest bit concerned. So was this an everyday occurrence in today's society? Was this level of utter degradation a perfectly normal event?

The general architecture of Santa Barbara is very attractive and has made the city a tourist attraction. We were only able to see a small part of it before it was time to start heading homewards. When we got back into the car the sun was shining but when we arrived in Moorpark a little over an hour later it was completely dark. And it was very noticeable that as the sun disappeared the temperature dropped quite rapidly.

Our journey coincided with the early evening build up of traffic. So once again we had the benefit of using the outside lane, the one reserved for vehicles carrying more than one person. But whereas in Washington they use the letters H.O.V. (high-occupancy vehicles), in California the letters painted on the road are C.P.O. I was told that these stand for Car Pool Only.

The build-up of traffic also meant that we encountered several examples of undertaking. (Is that a proper word? I use it to mean overtaking a vehicle on the inside.) You get into trouble for doing that in Britain but in America it's standard practice.

Arriving back in Moorpark we agreed that as it had been an energetic day it wouldn't be fair to expect Elizabeth to prepare an evening meal for us all. We would go out somewhere for dinner. Phil told us that not too far away was a restaurant renowned for its steak dishes and was appropriately named the Black Angus. A quick phone call reserved a table and off we went. I am quite partial to a good steak but when I saw the menu I quickly had other ideas. There was a really mouth-watering selection of fish dishes and my choice was halibut stuffed with crab and covered with cheese sauce. It was superb and I ate it slowly to try and make it last the whole evening. It was fascinating to see what types of fish are available in this part of the world, the eastern coast of the Pacific. I think a somewhat more leisurely day will be called for tomorrow after all the walking and eating today.

DAY 14

I was reading today about Juliette Low. What's that, you say? Never heard of her? No, nor had I until we came to the States. But that's only one side of the story. The other side is that very few Americans have heard of the name Baden-Powell. I'd better explain.

It was in 1907 that Robert Baden-Powell founded the Boy Scout movement. Its first big rally was held two years later at Crystal Palace and that was the historic occasion when some girls decided that they wanted to join in what was happening. They called themselves 'girl scouts'. So the following year, 1910, Robert's sister Agnes launched the Girl Guides Association. At that time Olave Soames was a very close friend of the Baden-Powell family and early in 1912 Robert married Olave.

They had an American friend, Juliette Low, who travelled to England to be a guest at the wedding. Whilst she was there she learned from Agnes and Olave about this new movement for girls and obviously their enthusiasm rubbed off onto her. She returned to her home in Savannah, Georgia, and telephoned her cousin in the same city. The result of that conversation was that the two ladies started America's first Girl Scout troop. They didn't use the name Girl Guides—to this day the movement is known as Girl Scouts. And the date of that phone call, 12th March 1912, is still treated with great reverence.

Robert and Olave shared the same birthday, 22nd February, and all over the world Scouts, Cubs, Guides and Brownies celebrate this date. It is known as Thinking Day because the aim is always to remember that this is a worldwide movement and to think about all those fellow-members in other parts of the world. I know that many people regard Thinking Day as the most significant date in the year for the two Baden-Powell movements.

The reason why I was reading about this subject today was that during the morning I was thumbing through a pile of books, pamphlets and leaflets. It was in this pile that I saw a book entitled *Forms Of Ceremonies For Girl Scout Units*. Glancing idly at the list of contents I noticed three or four alternative ceremonies for Founder's Day but only one small mention of Thinking Day. Founder's Day to Americans is 31st October which was Juliette Low's birthday (she died in

1927). I commented on this to Elizabeth and she told me how surprised she had been when she arrived in America to find that hardly anyone seemed to have heard of the name Baden-Powell.

D'you know, I have a feeling that in a way this seems to line up with what I had already noticed about the Yanks regarding America as the world. They acknowledge that somewhere back in the mists of time there were two people, Robert and Olave Baden-Powell, who in addition to being husband and wife also happened to have the same birthday. They include Thinking Day as a date on their calendars but it is only a 'minor festival'. They know that there are many Girl Scouts and Girl Guides in other countries but seem to assume that Juliette Low was the founder of an American movement that has now spread around the world. Elizabeth has received some disbelieving stares when she has tried to explain that the movement actually started in England and was very active some five years before it reached the States. I wonder if to many American minds it is inconceivable that any really good idea could originate elsewhere in the world and not in the States. Isn't any other nation given credit for anything?

After lunch we set out on a short trip, not too far and not too energetic. Corriganville Park, lying alongside the Simi hills, is a Western-style area of 246 acres which featured in many Hollywood films over the years. Elizabeth and Phil had a leaflet and so we had a chance to read something about it before we made our way there. The first thing I noticed was its address—7001 Smith Road, Simi Valley. Have you ever heard of a park having its own postal address? And as Smith Road turned out to be in the wide-open countryside with no buildings anywhere in sight, how did they come up with a number like 7001?

Let me quote a few extracts from the leaflet.

> *Ray Benard, born in 1902, entered films in 1932 as a stuntman and bit player. He became what is called a 'body double' for the Tarzan movie series starring Johnny Weissmuller. Later he changed his name to Ray "Crash" Corrigan. He progressed to becoming a star in serials and Westerns. By the early 1940's he was a producer and a few years later purchased this land which had been used for films such as 'Fort Apache', 'Riding With Buffalo Bill', 'Jungle Book', 'The Robe' and 'How The West Was Won'. It also featured in 'Lassie' and 'The Lone Ranger'. In 1949 he opened it to the public under the name of Corriganville Movie Ranch and ten years later it was attracting some 20,000 visitors each weekend.*
>
> *The park has not been used for filming since 1966. After Corrigan's death ownership passed to a Conservation Agency which was set up to purchase and maintain the area.*

It took us about half an hour to drive there and as soon as we arrived we could feel the atmosphere of the Wild West. As the four of us wandered along the dusty tracks we would from time to time hear a horse approaching. Round a bend would come a Park Ranger wearing full traditional cowboy outfit. We met three or four of these Rangers at different times; their task is to patrol the park and check that everything is okay. A bit like coppers on the beat. All of them were very cheerful and welcoming and quite happy to pause for a moment while we photographed them.

It was fascinating just to wander through the park and imagine what it had all been like during the halcyon days of the Hollywood films. In all the Tarzan films a popular shot had shown him diving off a bridge into a huge lake below. (From the leaflet we now knew that it was really "Crash" Corrigan.) We all stood on that bridge but didn't do any diving—it wouldn't have been a very good idea because after all these years the lake has dried up! I am told that a lot of people have called it the Tarzan Lake but nowadays the Conservation Agency refers to it as the Jungle Jim Lake. They say it's because the park was never used for complete Tarzan films but only for isolated shots like the diving scenes. Never mind—we could still stand on the bridge and let our imaginations run free.

And now what do you think of this for a coincidence? For those visitors who wish there are conducted tours led by a Park Ranger. We were making our own way around but we met up with one party that had some twenty or so in the group. As we passed we all exchanged greetings and the Ranger said, "You sound as if you come from England."

"Yes, you're quite right. We do."

"Gee. I've got an English lady in this group."

He pointed to a lady and I asked her, "Which part are you from?"

"Essex," she replied. "Colchester. Do you happen to know it?"

"Know it?" I said. "My wife and I were there a few weeks ago. We're from Southend and we took our young grandson to the zoo at Stanway."

There we were in this Western setting, five and a half thousand miles away from Essex. Mary and Elizabeth were both born in Southend and this lady told us she was born and grew up in Colchester before moving to the States. Honestly, it seems wherever you go in this world you'll find Essex Girls sooner or later. They get everywhere, don't they? This afternoon we had three of 'em together in the Wild West.

Corriganville Park is the kind of attraction that is known to American residents but wouldn't in all likelihood be on the list for overseas tourists. This was the advantage of our staying with someone who had local knowledge. It was great to visit places such as Gettysburg, Washington and Santa Barbara but we were getting just as big a thrill going to Fort Frederick, the pumpkin farm, the Chumash Centre and now this Park. In addition to seeing some of the tourist spots we were also going behind the glamour and getting a glimpse of the 'real' America.

It was proving to be a terrific holiday.

DAY 15

Ever since we have known Phil one of his favourite pastimes has been looking at new houses. If he goes anywhere near a new estate his instinctive reaction is to look for a show house. So this morning he took us to see some of the new developments in Moorpark.

The two houses where we had been staying, one in Maryland and one in California, were both open plan on the ground floor. Up until today we had not thought of this as being significant but now we realised that it is common practice in the States. Well, certainly with the modern houses. And in those parts of the country where the climate is hot they use tiled flooring extensively. It creates a cool and comfortable atmosphere. And the size of these new homes! Enormous. But I suppose when you have endless space available there is no need to economise on anything. The homes we saw nearly all had on the ground floor a large kitchen with a breakfast bar, a dining room, a lounge, a separate reception room and a television room. That's apart from the downstairs bathroom with large walk-in cloakroom. The 3-bedroom and 4-bedroom houses had all those bedrooms upstairs but where they were advertised as 5-bedroom we found that the fifth one was really a conversion of the downstairs reception room.

One interesting feature was the utility room. In British homes this is usually located adjacent to the kitchen and so it was with several of these American homes. But in others it was upstairs. Apparently the thinking is that upstairs is where you find most of the dirty linen and clothes and so it was more convenient to have the room there. I have not seen any houses in Britain with that arrangement.

The television rooms all featured the wall-type TV. You know, built into the wall with a screen roughly five feet square. More like a small cinema than a domestic room. And something which we all laughed about were the double beds in the master bedrooms. They were all six feet wide. Nearly half as wide again as a British bed. But thinking of the size of Americans whom we were seeing, Mary commented, "If you lie two Americans side by side they will need six feet. At least. Otherwise one of them will surely fall over the edge."

One aspect was, we thought, muddles thinking. Every master bedroom had its own en suite and a huge walk-in wardrobe. But in several homes we noticed that you have to walk through the en suite to get to the wardrobe. No problem if you are in the house alone, but surely it can easily happen that somebody wants an item from the wardrobe whilst somebody else is using the en suite. Sorry—nought out of ten for that idea.

Back home in the afternoon I was reading the newspaper when I spotted something that stopped me in my tracks. You probably know that in Britain our Scout Association and Guide Association each has a Royal Charter of which they are intensely proud, and rightly so. In America their Scout Association also has a Charter, though naturally not a Royal one, which reflects their status in the nation. Well, it appeared that there was a move gaining ground to have that Charter cancelled. It seemed to have been sparked off when a man applied to become a Scout leader and was turned down. The reason given for the refusal was that he had a record of sexual offences against young boys.

In the course of the ensuing arguments it was pointed out that the Scout Law includes a reference to Duty to God. Furthermore the Scout Association supports the traditional values of marriage and of family life. That was when the balloon went up. Atheists and agnostics immediately screamed that the Association is teaching intolerance because anyone who does not believe in God is being victimised. Then when Association leaders claimed to be fair-minded, this was promptly denounced as hypocrisy by advocates of homosexuality and single-sex marriages. Their argument was that if you say you approve of marriage between man and woman you are a hypocrite if you also claim to be fair-minded. You can't be, because you are discriminating against single-sex marriage.

I know that even Americans themselves admit that some strange things happen in their country but I reckon that this one takes the biscuit. Behind all the shouting and mud-slinging, there is what I regard as a crazy suggestion. It is that if you state an opinion on something—anything at all—you are automatically intolerant because you are discriminating against everyone who does not agree 100% with you. And you can only claim to be a fair-minded person if you never give an opinion on anything, because as soon as you do give one you will be practising discrimination, intolerance and victimisation. I wonder how all this will end up? We may never hear the outcome because it's the kind of news item that doesn't usually travel across the Atlantic. Personally, I don't think those who are kicking up the fuss will get their way in the long term. I believe this is one of those instances where the protesters and critics make lots of noise and grab all the publicity, but the silent majority just sit back until all the rumpus has died down and then quietly squash all the stupidity. I was already realising that in the States they have a silent majority of sensible, decent people just as we have in Britain. But in the meantime their Scout Association certainly has a fight on its hands.

As the Olympic Games were drawing to a close I read an announcement that some nations would like to include ballroom dancing in future Games. I suppose the theory is that anything which is competitive can be construed as eligible for a contest. It set me wondering what else we might consider in future. How about Olympic hop-scotch, Olympic scrabble or even Olympic limbo dancing? Then again, Olympic underwater yodelling?

Maybe we could give the musicians a chance and organise an Olympic bag-pipes contest. But no, on second thoughts that might encourage drug-taking. Among the audience, I mean, not the pipers.

The next concert by the Moorpark Symphony Orchestra was just three days away and so this evening Elizabeth had to go along to the final rehearsal. We other three just had a quiet evening at home. That's assuming that you can describe American TV as quiet. I was gradually becoming immune to the seemingly endless procession of adverts but there was also another point which irritated me somewhat. That was the overbearing music. Now don't get me wrong—I love music dearly. It's one of the great foundation stones of my life. But what I love is the right type of music in the right place. A lot of British TV adverts have music in the background but equally there are plenty of others with just the spoken word. In the States they seem unable to manage that. Every single advert has a musical background and in many instances it's not merely background. It is loud invasive music. To my mind it ruins the whole atmosphere of the advert and thus kills the message. Yes, I think you can assume that I was not exactly impressed by American TV advertising.

And have you ever heard of double news bulletins? What they do is have someone sitting in the TV studio reading and presenting the news as normal. But at the same time they run a tape across the bottom of the screen giving details of some other news item. So you really have to concentrate hard in order to absorb two quite different subjects simultaneously. I must admit that I found it difficult at first. But by the end of our holiday I had mastered the technique and when we returned to England I found our own news programmes quite tame by contrast.

DAY 16

The Queen Mary, one of the world's largest liners, was built on Clydeside and launched in 1934. For the best part of thirty years she sailed the popular Atlantic crossing between Southampton and New York, interrupted only by the war years when she saw service as a troopship. However, by the mid-60's commercial aviation had developed and was winning most of the business. In this increasingly frenzied world a seven hours flight was more appealing than a cruise lasting three days. Then in 1967 the Yanks hit on the idea of buying the liner and putting her on permanent show at Long Beach harbour. Long Beach is on the southern edge of Los Angeles and their harbour is the third largest in the world. (The other two are in China.)

Since arriving in California I had been saying I would like to see the Queen Mary. All right, you may laugh at the idea of travelling nearly a third of the way round the world to see something built just up the road in Glasgow. And Elizabeth told us that there was another attraction at Long Beach—the Aquarium of the Pacific. This was a fairly recent addition to the attractions of Los Angeles and I had not known about it. Thus after breakfast today we all set off for Long Beach.

We parked in a (free) multi-storey car park opposite the Aquarium and were immediately impressed by what a magnificent piece of architecture it was. (No, not the multi-storey!) The roof of the Aquarium is curved, shaped like rolling waves, and as the building is at the water's edge it almost seems to flow straight out of the ocean. The front is virtually all glass. It looked quite breathtaking in the morning sunshine; even more so in the early evening when all the interior lights were on. I have read that it cost $117 million to build.

As this was a Thursday I was surprised at the large number of people around. I noticed that many were Japanese—California is a popular holiday spot for them—and wondered if maybe their school year dates are different from the western world's. After all, we were now in early October.

Inside the main entrance is the Great Hall of the Pacific. High above us, suspended from the ceiling, was a full-size blue whale, the largest living creature in the world. Visitors were gasping in amazement but I felt quite blasé. "Oh no," I thought. "Not another blue whale. I've already seen one of them—in London at the Natural History Museum." But I decided it would be discreet to keep such thoughts to myself. Elizabeth immediately took a photo of the whale and in fact it turned out to be quite a good picture of the whole Great Hall. In the picture, standing immediately underneath the whale, are Mary and me, which gives a good indication of the size of the whale. But I'll let you into a secret. The real reason why we stood there was because right in the middle of the hall was one of those free-standing notice boards with a large arrow on it indicating the public toilets. She certainly didn't want that in the photo and got us to stand in front of it.

At the far end of the Hall against the wall is the most enormous display tank I have ever seen. Full of seawater, it must be some thirty feet high. It holds a lot of that underwater vegetation known as kelp, a kind of seaweed, and there are many various types of fish. But the big attraction is that there is also a diver in full kit. Inside his helmet he has a microphone which is linked to a loudspeaker in the Hall. He gives a commentary on what is happening all around him and tells us about those fish. Naturally this display was drawing a big crowd and it took me a few minutes to elbow a couple of small children out of the way.

The Pacific Ocean extends from the Bering Strait in the north to the Antarctic in the south, from Asia and Australia in the west to America and Canada in the east. Sometimes people are surprised to hear that this one ocean is almost as big as all the other oceans and seas in the world added together. The first European to sail it was the Portuguese explorer Ferdinand Magellan in 1520. In his language, the word 'pacific' means 'peaceful' and so he gave it that name because he found gentle and steady winds there.

I'm afraid this next paragraph will sound a bit like a catalogue but I want to tell you about the fish we saw on this visit. They were so completely different to anything I had seen previously in Sea Life Centres and, who knows, I may never see the like again in real life. As the Pacific is so vast this Aquarium is divided into three sections. In the Northern Pacific Gallery there were otters, giant octopus, spider crabs, rockfish and wolf eels. Moving into the Tropical Pacific Gallery we saw an exotic coral lagoon with blacktip sharks, sea horses, seasnakes, porcupinefish, puffers and angelfish. Finally in the Southern Gallery are examples of giant bass, leopard sharks, seals, turtles, sealions, guitarfish, halibut and stingrays.

It was all so thoroughly absorbing that we didn't realise how quickly the time was passing. But before we leave this wonderful Aquarium I must mention one amusing little fellow. He (I'm assuming it was a he—I'm not an expert on such delicate matters) was a seal pup playing with a pair of pliers. His home was a very tall tank. He was taking the pliers up to the surface of the water, letting them go and then diving to try and catch them before they reached the bottom. Sometimes he did, sometimes he didn't. We stood and watched for about five minutes—he was having the time of his life.

But now it was time for our next port of call. There is a network of transit buses around the harbour area and we caught one from the Aquarium to the Queen Mary. To our surprise this, too, was free of charge. When Americans come to Britain they must be quite taken aback at the many things we have to pay for here. Mind you, it was only a small single-decker and was entirely devoid of springs so I suppose it proves the old saying—you get what you pay for!

Before we go on board the liner here's a little story for you.

The ship was named Queen Mary due to a misunderstanding on the part of H.M. King George V. Cunard had intended to name her Queen Victoria, thus following the tradition of having the names of their ships ending in '-ia'. (Remember Britannia, Lusitania, Mauretania, Aquitania.) During his visit to Scotland a director of Cunard was asked by the King how the new ship was progressing. The director replied that all was going well and that the company hoped for permission to name her "after the most illustrious lady who has ever sat on the English throne". The King, supposing this to be a compliment to his wife, was deeply touched and answered, "I shall ask Queen Mary's permission."

All right, I'll come clean. It was established in later years that the story was quite untrue, without any foundation, just a figment of someone's imagination. But I couldn't resist including it for you to read. After all, it actually sounds quite plausible and it makes a good tale, doesn't it?

In Britain we expect senior citizens to be offered reduced admission prices to public buildings or for public events. In America this concession is also extended to past members of the armed forces. Here, as we approached the ticket booths for the Queen Mary, I noticed that they also offered reduced prices to serving forces personnel. In addition to selling you a ticket they also mark the back of your hand with an ultra-violet date stamp. As it is not visible to the naked eye I wonder how many times I washed my hands before it was finally gone. The idea is that you can leave the liner and then go back again as many times as you like on the same day without further payment. They simply check the back of your hand under their special torch. I mentioned to one chap there that in England we use 'pass out' tickets and he replied that you could pass those from one person to another and so get in without paying anything at all. Strange, that—I have already written that in several ways the Yanks seem more trusting than we Brits. Yet here was the reverse.

I suppose everyone has known the experience of looking forward eagerly to something and then finding that it didn't quite live up to expectations. The event sometimes does not match the anticipation. I'm afraid that our visit to the Queen Mary fell into that category. Elizabeth and Phil seemed very interested in all that we saw, but remember that they were both born in the late '60s by which time the liner's sailing days were over and she was on the point of being installed as a tourist attraction at Long Beach.

But Mary and I, we pair of geriatrics, were disappointed to find that the ship's interior has been to a large extent 'customised' (that's a respectable word for 'vandalised'). Much of the sharp end—sorry, the bow—was originally taken up by passengers' cabins. This area has now been converted into a 365-room hotel and was naturally out of bounds for us. We were able to glance into one dining room and one cocktail bar elsewhere on board, but without people in there they lacked any atmosphere. We could wander at will around the various decks and see the small hospital area. I think the shops are still as they always were but they are now called the Queen's Marketplace and sell rather tacky souvenirs for tourists.

In fairness, however, it was fascinating to look around such a gigantic ship. The sheer size is almost impossible to describe in mere words and I found it difficult to imagine this great bulk actually sailing across the ocean. Forgive me if I throw just a few statistics at you The ship was built to carry 1,957 passengers and 1,174 crew and there are two anchors, each weighing 16 tons. She was powered by four steam turbine engines of 40,000-horsepower each and the fuel consumption was—wait for it—13 feet to the gallon!! But here's my favourite statistic. Over her sailing years when she needed new coats of paint, what they did was just slap some more over what was already there. When she arrived at Long Beach they removed no less than 320 tons of old paint and this made her rise one and a half inches in the water. Then they applied just 8 tons of fresh paint ready for her new career.

The bit I enjoyed most was seeing the Captain's quarters and then going up onto the bridge. Here in the wheelhouse was the very nerve centre of this wonderful liner. I could imagine how the senior officers would have felt, standing here as they sailed into the great harbours of New York and Southampton. No, I hope I haven't given the impression that the whole of our visit was a disappointment. There was much to enjoy. It's just that I wish they had not been so heavy-handed with their 'updating'.

By the time we came away we knew that the evening rush hour would just be starting and so we decided to stay in the area and have a meal before tackling the journey home. We caught another of those transit buses, this time to a part of

Long Beach called Shoreline Village. This is a replica 19th century seaport area consisting of shops, bars and restaurants. We found a small restaurant which appeared to be just opening and on this early Thursday evening in October the proprietor seemed to be pleasantly surprised when no less than four customers walked in.

After the meal we walked around this Shoreline Village for a while—many of the shops were still open—but not for too long as it was almost dark and a strong wind had got up. Over the previous two or three days there had been weather forecasts threatening rain and indeed it did seem to be a possibility. So we caught another transit back to the Aquarium and made straight for our car. By now the worst of the rush hour was over and we only caught the tail end of it.

We had reached the northern edge of Los Angeles when it happened. It rained. No, seriously, that's headline news in southern California. In total we were there for four weeks and this was the very first time it had rained on us. It started suddenly and really did come down quite hard. A downpour, no less. It was bouncing up off the road. It carried on for about twenty minutes and then stopped just as suddenly as it had begun. And that was it. All over. Our holiday had almost another three weeks to go but that was all the rain we saw. 20 minutes in 28 days. No wonder so many Americans want to go and live in that part of the world and there are new homes going up all over the place.

DAY 17

This day of our holiday was partly devoted to Ronald Reagan. A remarkable man because during his life he scaled the heights, first in the acting profession, and then in international politics. He was born in Illinois, but it is California that features so prominently in his story. And I wonder if he is unique in that a museum was created in his name whilst he was still alive.

That was our destination today. It is in the neighbouring city of Simi Valley and its full title is the Ronald Reagan Presidential Library and Museum—a large building on top of a hill that makes it very imposing as you travel up the approach road. Parking facilities are free and that seems to be a regular feature of American life. Throughout our holiday in the States we only encountered very few instances where motorists have to pay for parking. It must be the usual business of unlimited space. Americans don't normally expect to be charged for parking—when it does happen it is the exception, not the rule.

Entering the building we found ourselves in a large foyer with the inevitable gift and souvenir shop to one side. But we could see that the far door led out to a balcony which offered a superb panoramic vista of the surrounding city and countryside. We stood and admired the view for a short while and then turned our attention to one of the museum's most historic items. Here on this balcony was a section of the Berlin Wall—you will know, of course, that it was during Reagan's Presidency that the wall was finally demolished. I estimate that this section measures about 6 feet wide by 20 feet high and it is totally covered with paintings and drawings. As it is such a precious exhibit it is naturally set well back so that it cannot be touched by visitors. I can still remember that famous day in 1989 when the wall was pulled down and the joy with which the news was received around the world. Today was another of those moments when I felt the significance of world history as I stood with a section of that wall right here in front of me. Another of those moments that make a mere human being feel very, very small.

As we had not left home very early it was already time to be thinking about lunch. I gather that for some time after this museum first opened there were no catering facilities. We saw signs indicating a cafeteria, followed them and found a small but compact café. They apparently didn't do major meals but it was just right for the snack we wanted. Being a little after midday on a Friday we didn't expect it to be crowded and, indeed, there was just one family ahead of us. The man was asking, "When did you open?" "Half an hour ago," they told him. It was only after a few more comments that we realised that this Friday was their very first day of trading. A brand new cafeteria. They really had opened, quite literally, half an hour ago! And I hope they do well because the food we had was excellent value.

Fed and watered, we returned to the main building to start our tour of the museum. Visitors have the choice of joining a conducted tour or making their own way around. We chose the latter. My own personal opinion is that sometimes these official guides have a tendency to rush you along and you don't have a proper chance to absorb all the details. So we wandered through the building under our own steam and found that as conducted parties were overtaking us we could listen to what the guide was telling them anyway.

I admit that in the past I had often wondered just why the American people had picked a film star to be their President. Today I found out the answer. I'll give you a quick bird's-eye summary of his life. He started his film career in 1937 playing very small roles but soon progressed to larger parts. Before long he was a star and it was around then that he met Nancy when she was also trying to build a career in films. They were instantly attracted to each other and this led to the marriage which he often described as the foundation stone of his life.

In those days the film industry was a wonderful world for the top names, but nowhere near so good for those lower down the scale. Ronald had a social conscience and started to campaign for better working conditions throughout the whole industry. He was soon an active member of a trade union, and because by then he had become so well known he was accepted as a leading negotiator. I have not seen anywhere any reference to a 'shop steward' but in today's language I suppose that's what he was in effect.

It was the experiences at this stage of his life that gave rise to an interest in political matters. He couldn't go on indefinitely in films as he had made his name in young, virile, athletic and romantic roles. Like a sportsman, he reached his sell-by date. So he turned to politics as a profession and very soon was elected Governor of California, the state which was the home of the film industry and where he had now settled with Nancy. The Yanks do go for famous names, don't they? Remember, earlier in this story, we were thinking about how they chose a professional soldier, General Eisenhower, to stand for election as President.

He was Governor of California for eight years. Towards the end of the 1970's the American economy hit a terrible period and it was obvious that President Jimmy Carter was not going to be re-elected. Ronald Reagan was invited to stand. He won the election and so 1981 began with his inauguration. But there was a near tragedy just a few weeks later. On 30th March, less than ten weeks after it began, his Presidency almost ended in violence. A gunman in the crowd shot at him, hitting him in the chest. Although the bullet was fired from a distance it missed his heart by just three inches. He staggered and a quick thinking Secret Service officer bundled him to the ground and lay on top of him for a moment. The incident sent shock waves through the nation—after all, this was less than twenty years after President Jack Kennedy had been assassinated.

He served two four-year terms as President and these are now known universally as the Reagan Years. The inauguration at the start of his second term was memorable because it was within days of his 74th birthday and he was thus the oldest man ever to be elected President. He became a tremendously popular leader and no, it wasn't just because people had known him as a famous film star. He had an engaging character, quietly spoken but with a ready smile. I have read somewhere that he used his storytelling abilities to make a point, deflect criticism and win over doubters. He would actually listen to other people's points of view, a very rare quality among politicians. It's not really surprising that our own Iron Lady, Margaret Thatcher, came over all girlish whenever she was with him and practically worshipped the ground he walked on.

Because of his personality there developed a great rapport between President and people. Over the years both Nancy and Ronald developed cancer and had to undergo major surgery. All over America there was a genuine upsurge of compassion and each of them said later that it had been a great source of comfort and support for them during such times of trial.

His greatest triumphs, of course, came in his dealings with the Russian leader Michel Gorbachev. Bit by bit progress was made in reducing east-west tension and, in addition to the pulling down of the Berlin Wall, the two leaders negotiated the signing of the 1987 INF Treaty. This was the first such treaty to do away with a whole class of nuclear weapons. Amendment 22 of the American Constitution stipulates that no President may serve more than two terms though a special exception was made during the Second World War for Franklin D. Roosevelt. So Ronald Reagan stepped down in January 1989.

There is one section of this museum that I was especially pleased to see. It is a full-scale replica of the Oval Office in the White House. I thought back a couple of weeks to when Mary and I had been there in Washington. The White House has four storeys. The ground floor consists for the most part of reception rooms and the next floor has all the state rooms. Next comes the floor with the Oval Office and the executive offices where the President's staff all work, and finally on the top floor, the penthouse, there are the family living quarters. During our visit we had been taken around the ground floor and state floor. So we had passed below the Oval Office and who knows, maybe in that fleeting moment the President himself might have been in the room immediately above us. It was fascinating for me now to stand and look at this exact copy of that most famous room. In a strange kind of way I felt that it somehow completed my visit to the White House.

These few short hours at the Ronald Reagan Museum made a thoroughly absorbing chapter in our holiday but there was one other experience that I must tell you about. In the corridor outside the replica Oval Office there is a small glass-fronted display panel on one wall. In that panel is a letter written by Ronald to the American nation—the original letter, not a copy. You see, after his departure from the White House he was diagnosed as suffering from the onset of Alzheimer's Disease. What an astonishing story his life had been. He achieved fame worldwide in the acting profession and later among international statesmen. Finally the crushing news that he was in the early stages of a devastating illness which would ultimately eat away his mind.

At that moment he sat down and wrote to his beloved American people. A simple two-page letter in his small handwriting. He told them how he treasured the honour of having been their leader and thanked them for having trusted him. He thanked them for having demonstrated their support and affection during the traumas of his cancer, Nancy's cancer and the assassination attempt. Now he humbly asked for their support once more—he told them about the Alzheimer's diagnosis. He did not seek support for himself, but for Nancy. He knew the full significance of what lay ahead and asked the nation to uphold her in their prayers. Eventually he would no longer understand what was happening to him but she would suffer the deepest pain.

The museum was not very busy that afternoon and there was nobody else in that corridor as Mary and I stood there reading the letter. I was glad of that because both of us felt it was the most emotional, the most humble letter we had ever seen. Without looking at her I knew she was as deeply moved by it as I was. After reading it we both stood there in complete silence for a few moments before turning and walking quietly away.

Back home for dinner and then this evening Elizabeth was going to a Girl Scouts meeting and she had invited Mary to go along with her. So now I'll hand over to Mary again to tell you about it.

◆   ◆   ◆

When Elizabeth was settling to life in America she hoped that her experience of Guiding would help her meet people and make new friends. Unfortunately, however, the first attempt did not work out.

She made herself known to the local association and they put her in touch with a Girl Scout leader who needed an assistant. For a time all seemed well—she was given a warm welcome by the leader, the girls and all the parents bar two. The problem was those two. "Why do we have to accept a woman from overseas in charge of our American girls? Why does she refer to our local group as having some kind of worldwide connections? And she admits that after several years of marriage she has no children, so why does she want to be involved in a children's activity? Has she got some kind of ulterior motive?"

The two of them started talking to other parents along these lines and gradually the atmosphere changed. The original welcome melted away. No one actually accused her to her face of having a hidden agenda but there was definitely a lot of whispering behind the backs of hands. Life in America is very much geared towards supporting your own children, not anybody else's. It is a self-focused nation in which the concept of helping the community comes lower on the scale of priorities than it does in Britain.

When Elizabeth realised why people had turned cool towards her and what cruel suggestions were being made about her motives, she was deeply hurt. She quit the post and told the local association what had happened. They were very concerned and took the matter quite seriously because indirectly it also reflected adversely on them. Now, before we arrived for our holiday, the association had contacted Elizabeth to tell her of another leader who needed help and assured her there would be no repeat of the previous episode. So this evening she was going along to that unit for the first time.

Both of us got a very enthusiastic welcome from the leader and the twelve girls there. It was their first meeting of a new term, a re-Dedication ceremony. In Britain we have Renewal of Promise when all units in an area come together for the occasion. In America their units function individually and have very little involvement with others. So the content of the ceremony is the same in both countries—it's the setting that's quite different. They had a cake with candles to represent the separate parts of the Scout Promise and Scout Law. Afterwards the rest of the meeting was spent in mapping out their programme for the coming weeks.

The meeting was held in the leader's home. This is standard practice in the States. They don't use church halls, school halls or community centres as we do in England. This put a thought into my mind. As the adults are interested only in their own children, what happens when the leader's daughter is old enough to leave? Does the unit lose a girl, a leader and a meeting place all at the same time? When Doug and I talked to Elizabeth about this later she agreed that indeed this is exactly what happens. Then along comes another leader, another mother with little (or maybe no) knowledge of Scouting and its history and traditions. No wonder the result is a lack of continuity. Now I see just how Elizabeth with her knowledge of campfire music and songs is teaching Americans something that they've never encountered before.

So American women are normally involved in Scouting for just a few years. We found, as we had at the training camp the previous week, general astonishment that Elizabeth had notched up almost 25 years in the movement. And I think it floored them completely to hear that my own membership is twice as long. But I must say again that they made us both very welcome and the first signs were that this time it would work out for Elizabeth.

DAY 18

We went to see a bit more of the film industry this morning. Along the freeway, about halfway to Los Angeles, we turned off and headed into the Santa Monica Mountains to visit the Paramount Ranch. It's an area of some 2,700 acres in the mountains and is still used by film and TV companies for location scenes. Films made here have included 'Have Gun Will Travel' and 'The Cisco Kid' and it has recently featured in the TV serial 'Doctor Quinn Medicine Woman'. Part of it is built up as a typical small township in the old Western days.

One caretaker-cum-security guard lives on site and I reckon he must be one of the loneliest men in the world. No neighbours for miles and miles in every direction. Fancy being able to play the *1812 Overture* as often as you like at full throttle with all the sound effects and nobody banging on the wall! The ranch is open to the public (something else free of charge) and some lucky visitors are able to watch filming in progress. We weren't. It was quite deserted today. During the hour or so that we were there the only human being we saw was a policeman—one of the highway patrol officers—who drove up, made use of the toilet facilities and drove off again. Still, I suppose there probably wasn't another loo for miles. I had already noticed that in America they don't appear to have services on the freeways as we do in Britain.

All the buildings were locked, of course, but we could let our imaginations have full rein as we wandered around, up and down the dusty streets, standing on the steps or verandas of shops, hotels, casinos and saloon bars. In future, whenever we see films or TV programmes with a Paramount label we will closely study all the outdoor scenes hoping to spot some familiar buildings. "Look, we've got a picture of you leaning on that handrail."

Back home for lunch, after which Elizabeth needed to do some shopping. Her two nearest supermarkets are Ralph's and Albertson's but this afternoon she took us to Wal-Mart, a little further away. This was interesting for us because Wal-Mart are expanding into Britain by taking over our Asda chain. We had thought that the Ralph's store was big, but golly—the Wal-Mart store was big, big, big. Not only do they sell food and clothing but also furniture, garden equipment and major electrical goods. All in this one store. Today Elizabeth stocked up with the necessary food and then she and Mary headed for the dressmaking and haberdashery section. Honestly, the selection of curtain materials alone was more than you would find in many specialist English shops.

What they were looking for was material to make a couple of fleeces. Mary would take the material and make it up when she was back home in Southend. A fleece for her was understandable as they are all the rage in England. But one for Elizabeth? Yes, it's because although the daytime temperature in California stays around the 80's it gets much cooler as soon as the sun goes down. It can drop quite quickly to the lower 60's and so a fleece is very useful in the evenings. So they sorted out two attractive lengths of material.

Outside in the car park (sorry, parking lot) I saw somebody pull into the area marked for handicapped drivers, get out of the car, then get back in and move elsewhere. Elizabeth saw me watching and commented that in the States they are very, very hot on this business of facilities for disabled drivers. If any able-bodied driver is caught using one of those reserved spaces then the authorities come down like a ton of bricks. None of the polite request to "move along, please" that we hear in Britain. Another example of the American philosophy that laws are drawn up to be obeyed and that nobody is above the law.

Mary and I were still quite surprised by the shortage of public transport in the U.S.A. There is a railway station in the city of Moorpark and in our naivety we had at one point suggested that to take some of the burden of so much driving off Phil and Elizabeth we might sometimes go into Los Angeles by train. But that was out of the question. Each day during the morning rush hour there are just five trains into L.A. and in the evening another five make the return journey. The population of Moorpark is about 100,000 and it is estimated that some 15,000 of them work in L.A. But obviously only around 3,000 of those travel by train; all the other 12,000 go by car. There is a railway line which runs all the way up the Californian coast from one end of the state to the other and the bit between Moorpark and Los Angeles is part of that line. But I gather that only three trains each day make the full panoramic journey and so although this is one of the famous lines in North America it is just single track. It's only at some of the larger stations that there are provisions for two trains to pass each other. Otherwise there is no need for a double track—there are hardly any trains. That's why, as I mentioned earlier, Mary didn't see a single train during our entire five weeks in America and I only saw one.

But on the subject of public transport, we spotted something unusual on our way back home. Each city seems to have its own domestic service, single-decker buses operating a circular route within the city limits. At one corner we saw a bus on the side of which we read, MOORPARK CITY TRANSPORT. POWERED BY NATURAL GAS. Now that could be a significant step forward, bearing in mind all these debates about pollution and global warming. We thought back to Ellen Bartlett's car in Washington—a hybrid car running on a mix of petrol and electricity and now a bus running on natural gas. Hello—maybe somebody somewhere is doing some serious thinking about the environment after all. Maybe all is not lost.

Anyway, back home for dinner, because this evening we were off to a concert. Time for a bit of Beethoven.

A few words about music in America. Elizabeth is a violinist and pianist and while she and Phil were still in England she worked as a violin and viola teacher. Her impression of U.S.A. music is that it is very much biased towards brass. Strings and woodwind music are almost second-class. The Yanks go for the big bands, the razzmatazz, the rah-rah majorettes. Plenty of noise. So although she found some work as accompanist to choirs, she has done hardly any violin tuition because few Americans are interested in that instrument

I have just looked at my latest copy of the publication *Music In South Essex*. Southend, with its 170,000 residents, has four orchestras, four operatic societies and ten secular choirs. By contrast Moorpark with 100,000 has just one symphony orchestra. Admittedly at the Moorpark College they have a jazz band and some chamber ensembles, but these are for students only. The symphony concerts are staged at the college and membership of the orchestra is drawn from local residents and college students. A number of them are obviously fine musicians, but not all. Elizabeth had warned me in advance that the standard was a fraction below what we expect from local orchestras in England. When she joined them they soon recognised her ability and she is now co-leader of the second violins. The conductor, James Song, is Head of Music at the college and in spite of his oriental name is 100% American.

The Performing Arts Centre at the college is an excellent concert venue. Ample platform space, good lighting and tiered seating, which means that everyone in the audience has a clear view. For this evening's concert I estimated the audience as about 200. That's not at all bad for a local concert and I was told that this is around the number they regularly get. Mary, Phil and I had arrived early and grabbed what we considered to be the best seats.

A full-size symphony orchestra is traditionally regarded as numbering 70 plus. For this evening's concert they had 54 and that included just nine in the woodwind section. A while back Mr. Song decided that over a period of a few years the orchestra would perform all nine of Beethoven's symphonies and this evening they had reached number six. That's the one usually known as the Pastoral Symphony. Personally I thought they played it reasonably well although a few of the woodwind entries sounded rather hesitant. I think that was because the shortage of numbers—only two clarinets and two oboes—probably affected their confidence a little. But I mustn't make this sound negative. Overall it was a careful, sensitive performance and clearly was understood and appreciated by the audience. They also gave us the first movement of the *Schumann Piano Concerto in A minor* with Suzanne Julian, a teacher at the college, as the soloist. Originally the intention had been to play the whole concerto but Suzanne's mother had died quite suddenly just a few days before the concert. It had been a great shock to the family and Mr. Song suggested they drop the piano item from the concert programme. But Suzanne didn't want to disappoint everyone and so they agreed a compromise, that she play just the first movement. Under the circumstances I thought she played brilliantly.

After the concert the orchestra and audience mingled in the refreshments room and once again Mary and I found ourselves the centre of attraction as guests from England. Several of the musicians were full of praise for Elizabeth's talent and told us they were looking forward to their next concert. "What a pity you won't still be here for that." They were going to perform Bach's *Concerto for Two Violins*, usually known simply as the Bach Double. A local professional violinist had agreed to be one of the soloists and Mr. Song had invited Elizabeth to be the other. The orchestra rehearses at the college on Thursday evenings and Mr. Song came up with a suggestion. "Would the two of you like to come along and sit in on our rehearsal next week? You will both be very welcome." I would love to have accepted his offer there and then. It had been a few years since we last heard Elizabeth doing any solo work. But we explained that on the coming Wednesday her older sister, Catherine, was due to arrive from England with her own two daughters. It was to be their first visit to America and as they would obviously be quite tired on the Thursday our plans for that day were a little uncertain. Elizabeth would certainly be at the rehearsal but the rest of us might want to spend the time quietly at home. So we left the invitation open as I still had the thought at the back of my mind that I might get along. I have always enjoyed listening to orchestral rehearsals (strange hobbies some people have!) because I can learn so much about the music from listening to the conductor's instructions and explanations. Then later when I hear it in a concert I hopefully understand the subtleties and nuances of the composition. Well anyway, that's the theory of it.

As a postscript to this evening I would just add one observation. The symphony concert was given only the very tiniest of mentions in the local newspapers. D'you know, I can't help thinking that this one fact in itself tells us something about the American approach to music.

DAY 19

It had been through Elizabeth spotting an advertisement in the local paper that we had visited that superb pumpkin farm. She did it again today—this time it was an Indian pow-wow. Over the centuries the number of Indians has decreased and most of those who are left have integrated into everyday American life. Across the entire 50 states I think the present number is less than two million. They dress and speak like other Americans and many are now very well educated. You can only identify them by their copper-coloured skin and jet-black hair.

But they greatly treasure their heritage and culture. Each year they organise a national pow-wow which lasts over a weekend and representatives from tribes all over the U.S.A. travel to take part. They choose a different venue each year and today it was being staged at the Live Oak Campground in Santa Ynez. This was a couple of hours' drive from Moorpark.

So yet again we were travelling the Pacific Coast Highway, this time north-westerly past Ventura and past Santa Barbara. The Sunday morning traffic slowed us down somewhat and it was almost lunchtime when we turned off the freeway onto a narrow road which twisted and turned climbing steeply into the mountains. We could easily have imagined that we had lost all contact with civilisation had it not been for two other cars some way ahead of us presumably aiming for the same destination. Finally, deep in the forest, we arrived at the campground. It was actually two very large clearings, one being used as a car park and the other as the showground. To start with we sat in the car and ate our lunch.

Then we walked through to the showground which consisted of a central ring, about 75 yards across, around which were ten large tents. Each tent was the base for one or two of the tribes. Beyond those were other, smaller tents in which were exhibited displays of handcrafts such as necklaces, jewellery, head-dresses, dream catchers, pottery, embroidery, ear-rings. It was really fascinating to wander around whilst we waited for the main event of the afternoon. The pow-wow had attracted several hundred visitors and the loveliest feature was that lots of Indians were mingling with the crowds. They were all wearing traditional dress, even the little children. It created a wonderful setting. (Though I was a little amused to see that a few of them were also wearing very 21st.-century spectacles.)

While we were doing this the drums were beating. I had noticed that on various posters there was an item reading DRUM CONTEST. ALL DRUMS WELCOME. P. A. SYSTEM PROVIDED. And boy, was that system effective! I don't know what the rules of the contest were but all the time we were walking around those drums were banging away and there was no escaping them. Never mind, it all added to the general atmosphere.

Then came the main event of the afternoon—the Grand Entry. The central ring was cleared and for the next hour members of all the tribes paraded. As each group finished their display they stayed in the ring and so it gradually became fuller and fuller which all made for rising excitement. Well, actually it was the drummers who seemed to be getting more and more excited and this communicated itself to everyone else.

Right at the start I was very impressed to see the Stars and Stripes carried in front of the parade. I wrote just now about Indians integrating into American life. It seems that all the violence and bitterness of previous centuries has finally been consigned to history and I could see that this afternoon the flag was carried with obvious pride and loyalty. It now takes place of honour at an Indian pow-wow.

Next in line came the Chumash representatives—as this is their part of America, or was, they were the host tribe and so paraded immediately behind the flag. As the ring filled it became a brilliant kaleidoscope of colour. All those taking part were dancing as the drummers reached near-frenzy. Finally we tore ourselves away from it all and went for one more look around those other tents. At one of them I bought an interesting map of the U.S.A. showing the locations of all the original tribes. I had never realised just how many there had been—I still haven't got round to counting all the names but there must be at least 150 of them.

Then it was back to the car as we had one further visit to make today. These are the Ojai mountains (pronounced oh-high) and we soon passed the huge Lake Cachuma in a valley. I have read that to the ancient Chumash people this valley and its lake were the spiritual centre of the world. We were headed now for the little township of Solvang some twenty miles away.

The name Solvang is Danish and in that language the word means 'sunny valley'. The town was established in 1911 by immigrants seeking a quiet pastoral spot in which to establish a folk school. They settled on this Mojoqui Falls County Park (pronounced mo-ho-wee.). Buildings, parks, everything is in the Danish style. Right in the centre of town is the old Mexican mission of Santa Ines and we found a spot nearby in which to park. For the next hour or so we had a delightful time walking around.

It's a Danish oasis in sunny California. Half-timbered houses with thatched roofs, a working windmill (in Hamlet Square), restaurants, galleries and endless bakeries and gift shops. In the centre of Main Street is a monument to, guess who, Hans Christian Andersen. There is also a Lutheran church where some services are conducted in Danish. To this day more than two-thirds of the residents are of Danish descent.

One shop in particular sticks in my memory. The most enormous selection of cuckoo clocks you could ever imagine. Right along one wall, the full length of the shop. You should have heard the uproar when they all struck the hour! Another shop, named the Candy Barrel, had some confection called Saltwater Taffy. We didn't pluck up the courage to try that but I admit that we sampled the Danish ice cream and pastries. That slowed us down a bit.

I picked up one little snippet of information. In Santa Barbara, about thirty miles away, they will tell you that is where Ronald and Nancy Reagan used to vote at election times. Not so. The Reagans' home was between the two towns but actually slightly closer to Solvang. So when there was an election they used to drive into Solvang and record their votes there in a local school hall, just like all the other citizens (but in fairness I think the postal address of their home was Santa Barbara.)

It was quite a long drive back to Moorpark and well into the evening when we arrived and we decided to eat out But it was a Sunday evening and the first restaurant we tried was fully booked. Our second attempt was an Italian restaurant and they had a couple of tables spare. Do you know, it was a brilliant meal. I hope it doesn't sound disloyal of me but we visited several restaurants during our weeks in the States and although the meals were all enjoyable I have to say in all honesty that this Italian meal was the best. Sorry about that, you American chefs.

And a few months later I could still hear those perishin' drums hammering away!

DAY 20

A quiet time today, pottering about. Just as well because our holiday in California was proving quite hectic and we needed time to draw breath occasionally. Furthermore, in a couple of days' time our other daughter, Catherine, would be arriving with her two girls and they would be wanting to rush around seeing as much as possible. The one who didn't get a rest today was Phil because during the morning he had a phone call asking if he could go into the office for an hour or two.

Mind you, Mary and I were awake early today. I have already referred to the fact that in America mornings begin earlier than in Britain. Well, there is a small zoo not far from where Elizabeth and Phil live and right at the start of our four weeks there they warned us that each morning we might hear the gibbons shouting as their breakfast time approached. Yes, we did hear them several times but it was not in any way an intrusive noise. After all, we've known a few humans shouting for food before now. Good luck to the animals—at least we knew that they were properly fed and well cared for. It is in fact a small training zoo where students learn their profession.

But this morning was different. A little after 7 o'clock the next-door neighbour was out with his lawn mower and hard at it—getting his lawn all neatly mown before he went to work. And yet when we had met him a day or two previously he had seemed such a nice chap!

We had had four busy days in a row and so welcomed a relatively quiet time today. In the morning we went shopping in Simi Valley. An unusual name, isn't it? I did a bit of research. It seems that the name is derived from the original Chumash village Shimiyi. It remained a very minor township until around 1900 and was still primarily a farming community until the growth of the film industry in the 1920's. Then people realised that it was a pleasant place to live within fairly easy reach of Hollywood. But it was in the 1970's, with the construction of local freeways, that there was a population explosion to the present level of some 100,000. There, as in Moorpark, a great deal of building work is under way as still more and more people are flocking to make their lives in this corner of the States.

We visited what I think is the largest toy shop I have ever seen, keeping an eye open for anything suitable for grandchildren. When I found one item I took it across to the cash desk where another customer was being served. "Come back, Dad," said Elizabeth. "Stand here." I didn't understand what she was getting at and so she explained. In America never 'close up' a queue. While the person at the front is being served the second one should stand no closer than about six feet away. If this was meant simply as a protection of privacy I could understand it and I think I approve. But in fact she said the reason is that Americans regard it as a form of aggression if one person stands immediately behind another. Personally I find that amusing because although I like the Yanks I think they are a bit 'pushy' and I know that many people share that opinion. The truth is that they are all very proud of being American and they want the whole world to know it. Yes, they do make a lot of noise about it but they can't understand why anyone should be surprised by their attitude. What makes me smile is that such extrovert and demonstrative people get uptight at the mere thought of anyone simply standing just behind them.

I wonder what life in Britain would be like if some of us were brave enough to declare openly that we are proud of being British. Perhaps if we flew the Union Jack outside our homes. Most likely we would find ourselves the object of public ridicule. Nowadays it is fashionable to grab every chance of decrying our nation. Our so-called comedians on radio and television get most of their laughs from knocking Britain. D'you know, I think these few weeks in America did me good. A month or more among people who are proud of their country and regularly say so. It was an unusual and lovely experience.

In another shop I noticed a blind man having difficulty with his small change and the assistant was helping him. I could sympathise because American coins are a bit confusing. In descending order they are 25 cents, 10, 5 and 1. But the size of the coins does not decrease in that same order. The 10 cents is smaller than the 5. This nearly caught me out during our first week but then I came up with the idea of keeping my 10 cents coins in a separate pocket. After that it was easy but I do certainly feel sorry for their blind people.

We took the scenic route from Simi Valley back to Moorpark, the long way round via Thousand Oaks. Elizabeth wanted us to experience what she considers the world's greatest ice cream parlour. (And don't forget that we Southend folks know a thing or two about ice cream.) I can't remember its name but what they do is offer you an extensive choice of flavours, quite a generous scoop. With that they mix in some fruit of your choice and then top the lot with shredded nuts. My selection was ice cream of a mild peppermint flavour mixed with small pieces of black grape and topped with shredded walnuts. It was a banquet—no other word for it.

My most pleasant memory of this morning was the ubiquitous "You're welcome". In every shop you visit everybody says it. And the important thing is that they mean it, they really do. As you walk into any supermarket or big store a member of staff calls out a welcome. They are genuinely pleased to see you. Occasionally they even have somebody just standing there at the doorway to welcome you and thank you for visiting them. And while you are there, if you speak to a member of staff about anything at all they always end the conversation with "You're welcome". I had gone to America believing that at the cash desks all the cashiers would tell me to "Have a nice day". Well, throughout the holiday only two or three did—everyone else told me "You're welcome".

Back home we were unloading our purchases when I could swear that I felt a slight shudder underfoot. It was only the tiniest of movements and nobody else appeared to notice it. But being in California one thought immediately came into my mind—earthquakes. It was all over in a split second and I wondered if it was really just my imagination.

We had not seen rain since flying across the States but this afternoon there were some ominous clouds. Elizabeth told us that on those few occasions when it rains in southern California it comes down quite heavily and usually with little warning. She said that local people talk about their year being split into four FRED seasons—Flood, Rain, Earthquake, Drought. I think I would rather stick with Spring, Summer, Autumn, Winter.

In the afternoon I took the opportunity to watch some 'foreign' television. British, for example. You can get upwards of sixty channels on the normal American TV and included in all that lot is one, just one, British channel. I switched it on out of idle curiosity. Lo and behold, I found myself watching the Antiques Roadshow.

After that finished I flicked around the sports channels until I found a football match. This one was from South America which, of course, was not actually all that far away. An international match, Columbia versus Paraguay, and for my money the man of the match was the referee. You know how excitable some South Americans can be. Well, when the Columbians scored their players went bananas. They were jumping and dancing around for some two or three minutes until the ref got fed up with it. To my delight he lined up the Columbian team and dished out no less than *seven* yellow cards for time wasting. I thought he was great and wanted to give him a medal. Why don't the British refs clamp down on some of those prima donnas in our game?

On a more serious note I also listened to part of a debate between evolutionists and creationists. I didn't remember the significance of those names at first until the programme began. The evolutionists believe that the world as it is today has evolved over many millions of years. They say that human life is the latest stage in a process that began with fishes and developed later through many stages of vertebrate creatures and animals. I had always assumed that this belief is universally accepted nowadays as it is backed up by hard evidence. But no. The creationists believe that the Biblical story as set out in the first chapter of Genesis is literally true—that the world was created in just six days together with all forms of life as we know them today. The debate, part of which I heard today, is over what should be taught in American schools. The creationists are demanding that children (even non-Christians!) be taught that the Bible is infallible, the Word of God, and therefore the Genesis explanation is completely true. They denounce the theory of evolution as the work of Satan. They classify all the historians, archaeologists, geologists, astronomers, etc. as slaves of the Devil. I wonder how this dispute will end up. At this stage neither side seems willing to give an inch.

We finished up with a relaxing evening at home. A few games of pool, a bit of TV, some reading of the local newspapers and just general chit-chat. Looking ahead to the arrival of Catherine and her two daughters, Chloe and Emily, we agreed that we would spend three days at Disneyland by booking a couple of nights at one of their hotels. A session on the telephone soon sorted that out though we found that prices are quite high. Now I see what the local folks mean when they say that Mickey is a very greedy little Mouse.

However, what was not so successful was the attempt to book a tour at the Universal film studios. All they could offer was a tour starting at 9 a.m. But that would mean seven of us getting dressed, fed and watered and out of the house by around 7.30. No way. Surely there are other tours during the day? Yes, we were told, but places on those are reserved for the concierges of the many Hollywood hotels. When they have taken their pick for their customers there are rarely any spaces left for the general public. So we reluctantly had to cross that one off our list of planned visits. I suppose you can't win 'em all.

DAY 21

J. Paul Getty was reputedly one of the world's richest men and during his lifetime amassed a staggering collection of artistic treasures. Paintings and drawings by Van Gogh, Monet and Michelangelo, sculptures, Chinese pottery, illustrated manuscripts from the Middle Ages and the Renaissance, classical furniture and musical instruments—you name it, he had it. At his death in 1976 he left the whole collection to the nation plus $700 million (most of his estate) in order to house it in a public museum. One was established, using some of the money, at Malibu, but it was always felt that such a sensational collection deserved an equally sensational setting. With that aim in mind the rest of the money was invested and thus in 1998 a new Getty Centre was built on the northern side of Los Angeles at a cost of $800 million. This new Centre was our destination today. It turned out to be the most amazing museum I have seen or could ever hope to see. Even now my spine still tingles as I think back to that day. I will always remember that feeling of awe which almost took my breath away.

It is built on the side of a mountain. From the freeway we drove along a short approach road leading to a multi-storey car park where they charge five dollars per car irrespective of how many people are travelling in it. Beyond that there is no further admission charge. The 6-level car park is underground, built into the mountain. What do you think of that? A multi-storey car park entirely underground. Some lifts convey visitors from the various levels back up to the surface, which is at the bottom of the mountain level with the freeway. From here there is a computer-controlled monorail tram service up the side of the mountain to a station at the top.

This is on one side of the arrival plaza from which there are panoramic views across L.A. to the Pacific on the horizon and, in the other direction, of the mountains all around. The museum consists of five large pavilions, separate buildings linked by walkways. Everything is built of imported Italian travertine marble, 16,000 tons of it. That is the same marble as was used to build the Coliseum, the Trevi Fountain and the colonnade of St. Peter's Basilica. There is also a restaurant, two cafes, a 450-seat auditorium and a library with more than 700,000 volumes. All this on the side of or on top of the mountain! Seen from down on the freeway it looks like some fairy-tale medieval castle high above the city and ocean. One reaction from an Australian visitor has been recorded—"If God had the money this is perhaps what He would have done."

After admiring the view we decided that before going inside the buildings we would look around the gardens. Yes, gardens on top of a mountain. The crowning glory is the Central Garden, which is actually planned in the shape of a hand-held mirror. The 'handle' is created by an echo-chambered stream flowing downhill and flanked by flowering plants and a canopy of myrtle and plane trees. At the bottom the stream cascades over a stepped stone wall and opens out into a reflecting pool surrounded by azaleas. Unfortunately late September and early October is not the time to see azaleas at their best—the garden surrounding this pool must be absolutely stunning when they are in full bloom.

There is also a second, smaller garden named the Cactus Garden and we went to see it. It is marked on the leaflets and pamphlets but very little information is given. I wonder why. Perhaps it is because local people see cacti every day of their lives and think of them as being hardly worth a second glance. But to Mary and me they were a novelty and we were very impressed by the number of different varieties in this garden. One snippet of information I did glean was that in this ultra-modern creation cacti have been included to mark the pre-urban state of this part of the United States. A link with ancient history—quite appropriate for a museum, really.

Finally, before going into the pavilions, we patronised one of the cafes. Good food at a reasonable price. But what I liked best was that next to the boxes holding the clean cutlery were two large bowls full of peppermint sweets. Just help yourself, no charge.

Once we started going around the actual museum it was absolutely staggering. Paintings from many different centuries, sculptures, displays of photographs showing progress from the very earliest efforts right through to the latest technology. We gasped at damask-covered walls, huge tapestries, beautifully carved furniture of many genres and elaborate mirrors. We wandered through room after room packed with ceramics, decorative glassware, Greek and Roman artefacts. Elizabeth and I both drooled at the collection of ancient musical instruments. To give you an example of the lengths they have gone to—in the galleries where they have paintings there is a computerised system of louvered skylights which allow natural light to filter in and so give as close as possible an approximation of the conditions in which the artists painted.

Over the years my own experience has been that the major museums can easily be a bit daunting. There is so much to see, so much to try and absorb. One visit cannot really be sufficient. I think there comes a point when one's head says, "That's enough—I can't take any more." Mary calls it brain-ache. That was the stage we all reached after a few hours at this almost unbelievable Getty Centre. I think that to get maximum appreciation from this museum you would have to make separate visits to each of the pavilions and spend maybe two or three hours in each one. Otherwise you reach the same stage as us, where you read the notices and explanations but somehow it just doesn't register. But don't get me wrong—I wouldn't have missed this visit for the world.

One abiding memory of this Centre was the absolute cleanliness. Maybe the fact that so much is marble is a help. I imagine someone giving it a quick rub down with a damp cloth. But seriously, it was spotless. I realise that it had only been opened just a few years before we were there and so there hadn't been time for it to become dowdy. We were lucky to see it in almost pristine condition. It had been the same story when we were at the Aquarium of the Pacific. That, too, had been built around the same time and so we saw it before it could show any signs of wear.

We made our way back to Moorpark in the late afternoon but didn't have a meal at home as we had been invited to a barbecue. It was organised by a Girl Scouts company and so everyone assembled at one of those public barbecue sites. While the food was being cooked the father of one of the girls gave a talk on Hiking and Overnight Camping. He had brought quite a selection of gear with him and so was able to show the girls just how to use it.

Mary and I sat quietly at the back of the group and found it absolutely fascinating. Remember that these girls live where the Santa Monica Mountains are within easy reach and so hiking there is a different world from hiking in Essex or Kent. The wildlife there can be literally wild—how would you like a large bear sniffing all round your tent in the middle of the night? There are designated routes over the mountains but sometimes they are merely dust paths and not always easy to follow. All this calls for somewhat different equipment from what our British hikers use and different protective clothing. He demonstrated, for example, how to purify water taken from a mountain stream and also how to deal with snakes inside a tent.

There were a number of parents who had come along to help with the meal and all of them gave Mary and me a great welcome. The father who had given the talk was very pleased to tell me he had visited England twice, but yet again it transpired that the only place he had been to was London. I suspect that it did his street cred a power of good in front of the other parents when he and I talked about places we both knew—Buckingham Palace, the Tower, Piccadilly Circus and, of course, Harrods. Every American goes to Harrods.

And it wasn't just the parents who gave us a welcome. For some of these young girls, living over on the far side of the U.S.A., we were maybe the first real British people they had ever met. They gazed at us as if we were characters from a book who had suddenly come to life. I remember especially one very little girl, possibly the youngest one there. Her mother told us that the girl absolutely idolised the memory of Princess Diana. She collected pictures, newspaper cuttings, trinkets, souvenirs, magazines, anything else she could find with some reference to Diana. She called the girl across to us and told her, "This lady and gentleman come from England, the same country as Princess Diana." The girl's eyes opened wide and she seemed so thrilled that she couldn't speak for a few moments. (Mind you, I do sometimes have that effect on little girls—it's the big ones who look at me and walk away!)

In true American fashion there was a mountain of food at the barbecue and we could easily have eaten ourselves to a standstill. What with all the talking and eating I didn't notice how time was passing until I glanced at my watch and saw it was seven o'clock. Surprisingly it was quite dark. That's something that's characteristic of this part of California. Blazing sunshine all day long but then the sun goes down quickly and within minutes—or so it seems—everything is very dark. There is none of the gradual dusk which we know in England. And at the same time the temperature drops significantly. Before leaving England we had joked about this, saying that in California they shiver when the temperature drops to 70. But once we were there we found that wearing a fleece when you go out in the evening is a good idea.

At the end of the meal it was interesting trying to pack away the utensils and any food which was left over. That's because I think they had expected it to finish before darkness descended and only one parent had brought along a flashlight (the American word for a torch). We think that we finally got everything packed in the correct bags and boxes before we all made off in our respective cars.

Back home Elizabeth showed us a video recording she had kept from the previous New Year's Day. The Tournament of Roses Parade in Pasadena which is a suburb of Los Angeles. It is apparently a huge annual event on 1st January. Dozens of floats all decorated with flowers, goodness knows how many bands, street entertainers, majorettes, equestrian displays. And thousands, honestly thousands, of Stars and Stripes everywhere you looked. I've seen some pretty good carnivals and processions in my time but this one left them all standing. The TV commentators were telling us it took four hours for the parade to pass any one spot and so the video lasted that long. It was brilliant, superb, but we didn't stay up to watch the whole lot.

DAY 22

I must tell you about a family named Griffith. When Mr. and Mrs. Griffith had a son, guess what Christian name they chose for him? Griffith! Seriously, I'm not joking. The poor chap had to go through life telling everybody that his name was Griffith Griffith. Oh, honestly, the thickness of some parents is almost breathtaking. Anyway, the point is that he became a very rich man; at his death in 1935 he owned 4,000 acres of parkland and forest on the north-eastern edge of Los Angeles at the foot of, and partly up the side of, the Santa Monica Mountain. In his will he left the whole lot to the city of L.A. and inevitably they named it Griffith Park. That was where we were heading for today.

Griffith Park in Los Angeles reminded me of Hyde Park in London. The scenery was very different, of course, but I'm referring to the atmosphere of gentle tranquillity. It was difficult to realise that we were quite close to the centre of one of the world's major cities. On this beautiful sunny day the park was a haven of birds, squirrels and general serenity. Mind you, I have heard that after dark it then becomes a haven of drugs and homosexuality but I closed my mind to that. We wandered around the park for a while and then drove up the hill to the park's crowning glory, the Griffith Observatory and Planetarium.

In the States they do have this sense of the highly dramatic, especially with regard to major buildings. The Capitol in Washington, the Ronald Reagan Museum, the Getty Centre and now the Griffith Observatory—all of these are situated on the tops of hills or mountains. As you approach them they tower above you and are so awe-inspiring. This observatory is a large white stucco building topped by three copper domes and from the roof terraces there is a stunning panoramic view of the city.

But looking in the other direction, towards the mountain, there is another view which is a 'must' for every tourist. That world-famous HOLLYWOOD sign in big white letters. You've all seen the picture in travel agents' brochures. The history is that it was erected in 1923 by estate agents when the area was first developed. The letters, made of sheet metal painted white, are 50 feet high and it originally showed HOLLYWOODLAND. Following vandalism the last four letters were removed in 1949 and a security fence installed.

But I'll let you into a secret. The pictures you have seen all show the letters against a dark green background, hundreds of trees and bushes. Not so. Elizabeth took a photo of Mary and me, including the sign away in the distance—proof that we really did go to America and I haven't simply dreamt up everything you've been reading. But the background is not dark green. Oh yes, the trees and bushes are there, but in the picture they come out as dark grey. That's because Los Angeles, maybe on account of its unbelievable, never-ending traffic congestion day and night, has the worst pollution record of any city in the world. I know that those trees, about two miles away, really were green but the grey colour in the picture is actually two miles of pollution. So don't believe everything you see in brochures.

This should have been of great concern to me. I occasionally suffer slightly from asthma and so before we left England I carefully included an inhaler and a few tablets in our luggage. I was naturally hoping not to need them but the prospect of four weeks in the L.A. area meant that I couldn't be too careful. Well, in the event I didn't use them at all—carried the whole lot back home again. Down at ground level the air quality gave me no problem at all and in fact I had forgotten all about pollution until today as we stood outside the observatory and looked across the valley at the big HOLLYWOOD sign. At that moment it brought home to me just how bad the situation really is. For the first time in my life I could actually see aerial pollution. I thought back to a line I once read in a magazine:

I shot an arrow in the air—and it stuck!

Then we moved inside the building. It could easily sound a bit dismissive to say that every planetarium shows basically the same exhibits. Over the years I've visited a few but this one in L.A. has some unique items. For a start the entrance hall houses a large pendulum. Bear with me for a moment while I quote from the official description.

> *This pendulum gives direct proof that the earth rotates on its axis. It is a 240-pound brass sphere suspended from a 40-foot steel wire. A ring magnet above the ceiling keeps the pendulum in motion without influencing the direction of its swing.*
>
> *Under the pendulum stands a circle of pegs. Every ten minutes or so the pendulum knocks another one down but it is not the pendulum that has moved over to hit the peg. The earth has moved it into the path of the swinging pendulum which is essentially disconnected from the turning of the earth. Once started in*

motion the pendulum continues to swing in the same direction regardless of what the earth does. It is actually the rotation of the earth which makes it look as if the pendulum is changing the direction of swing.

Sorry if that all sounded rather technical but it was a totally absorbing demonstration. I confess that more than once while we were there we nipped back to the entrance hall to see if any more pegs had been knocked down yet. (Some people never grow up!)

It was natural that an American planetarium would make a great fuss of their national space programme. It was an impressive display as was also the replica of the Hubble space telescope.

However, one section in this building made me stop and ponder. Earthquakes. The situation is this. Most of California teeters on the western edge of the vast North American Plate. The adjacent Pacific Plate, which first collided with what is now California about 250 million years ago, grinds slowly but steadily northward along a line which we call the San Andreas Fault. Plate movement is usually imperceptible but at the present rate Los Angeles will slide north and become San Francisco's next-door neighbour in about 10 million years' time. Every year now there are around 15,000 movements. The overwhelming majority are barely noticeable but they are all technically earthquakes.

My thoughts immediately went back a couple of days to when I was helping unload the car and felt a slight shudder underfoot. Nobody else had noticed it. Imagination? It could have been but now I'm not so sure. 15,000 a year equals 1,200 during our four weeks in that part of the States. Twelve hundred!! Yes, I'm convinced it was a minor earthquake I felt that day.

Next came an important point in our holiday. While we were spending an enjoyable few hours at this park and planetarium our other daughter, Catherine, with her own two daughters, Chloe and Emily, was somewhere in mid-air between Heathrow and Los Angeles. Their scheduled arrival time was 8 p.m. At 4 p.m. Phil said it was time to leave the park and head for the airport ten miles away.

What? Four hours to travel ten miles? Yes, because one thing we had to do before meeting the others was collect a second vehicle. For the rest of the holiday there would be seven of us and so we would be hiring a 4 x 4 people carrier, or S.U.V. as the Yanks call it (sports utility vehicle). To reach the airport we had to travel through the centre of L.A. in the early evening traffic and it did indeed take us two hours to travel those ten miles. Then when we arrived at the car hire centre all the formalities ate up another half hour of our budgeted time. From there we made our way to an airport car park, Phil driving the people carrier and the rest of us following in the car.

You'll remember that when Mary and I flew to L.A. from Washington we arrived at terminal 7. This time we were meeting a transatlantic flight and they use terminal 1 which I thought was, quite frankly, a rather dowdy building. The whole structure looked somewhat elderly, the furnishings were a bit sparse and the quality of lighting was not the best. Anyway, we found a snack bar where the food and drink were passable though barely worth the prices they charged. But I mustn't be too critical because the airport operators gave me one good laugh to brighten up the wait. There is a big problem in American cities with beggars—they have no shame in pestering people quite openly. So here at L.A. Airport there was an announcement repeated over the loudspeakers every ten minutes or so. "We are aware that people are moving around these buildings soliciting money. Please be advised that you should not give money to solicitors." Okay, I'll go along with that. I've grumbled more than once about the fees which solicitors charge. So how do they feel in L.A. about architects, accountants and estate agents?

Catherine and the girls had taken off from Heathrow at around 5 p.m. Wednesday evening and flown for eleven hours. So when they landed at Los Angeles their body clocks were telling them it was 4 a.m. Thursday morning. But because of the time difference it was in fact only 8 p.m. Wednesday in L.A. They landed on time but we had to wait in the arrivals area for another three-quarters of an hour before they came into view trundling their luggage. Catherine and Chloe both looked as if they were sleepwalking; Emily seemed quite perky but I wondered if perhaps she was on autopilot.

The drive back to Moorpark took well over an hour because even in late evening the traffic around Los Angeles never completely eases off. Phil had his first experience of driving the people carrier on the freeways and appeared to be enjoying himself. Back home our new arrivals suddenly realised how tired they were and couldn't get to bed quick enough. Tomorrow would be a fairly quiet day to let them get over their jet lag, but then beyond that there were going to be some exciting days ahead.

DAY 23

Not surprisingly it was around 10 a.m. by the time Catherine, 13-year old Chloe and 11-year old Emily were all vertical again. So after a leisurely breakfast we went out for our first experience of all riding together in the people carrier (which we immediately nicknamed 'the bus'). Phil drove. The original intention had been that the driving would be shared but in the end it turned out that he drove it all the time. We think he was quite pleased at being in control of this large powerful vehicle. Monarch of the road, and all that…

We went to Ralph's supermarket. Catherine and the girls were just as amazed as Mary and I had been by the sheer enormity of the place. They wandered around the aisles with eyes like organ stops. And on this their first visit to America they had only been in the country for a little over twelve hours when there was a memorable moment for all of us.

Two ladies doing their routine shopping heard our English accents and paused to speak to us. They thanked us profusely for the way in which Britain supported America in Iraq. Their gratitude stopped us in our tracks—it was almost overwhelming. They spoke, they said, not just for themselves but for the vast majority of decent American citizens. We told them that back in Britain most people felt the action to remove Saddam Hussain was justified. Most, but not all. We had a significant minority who protested that the action was wrong. I had already learnt from Maury that there was a similar range of opinions among Americans. But these ladies were also aware that some nations were highly critical of America's decision to topple Saddam, whereas the Brits had stood alongside the Yanks from day one. Now here, in the middle of a busy supermarket, we ordinary folks were being greeted like heroes as if we had just saved the world. It was so unexpected and made us feel surprised, honoured, thrilled, humbled, all at the same time. What an introduction to the United States for our three new arrivals.

As we came out of the shop Emily asked me why there was a sign saying Leave Carts Here. From my (after three weeks) fluent mastery of the American language I was able to explain that what Americans call carts are what we British know as supermarket trolleys.

Back home for a light lunch and then out again for a general drive around the district. I found this an intriguing afternoon because I saw California afresh through the eyes of three newcomers. They noticed and mentioned things that I was already taking for granted—the citrus groves, the tall slender cypress trees, the ubiquitous cacti. Catherine was captivated by the variety in styles of architecture. When we humans encounter something new isn't it strange how quickly we then accept it as being routine? Mary and I had been in California for only two weeks yet already our minds were accepting everything around us without question, without comment. This afternoon we were discovering it all over again. An example of this was when Mary pointed up at the hills towering over us and exclaimed, "Oh look. The purple-headed mountain." Yet she and I had already travelled along that road three or four times on previous days.

And it was nice to have a couple of youngsters with us who were taking an intelligent interest in this new experience. Their two schools had agreed to the request for time off on the basis that learning about America (from the inside, in a sense) was a valid step forward in their education. In Emily's case I think they had already said that they would like her to write a project on California when she arrived back in Kent.

We learned something about car number plates today. It started when we noticed a car ahead of us with the registration plate BUSH 4 ME. Was that legal, we wondered, even for an enthusiastic supporter of the Republican Party? Yes, we were told, because across America the laws governing number plates vary from one state to another. In California the ruling is that each registration must contain seven digits of which at least one must be a figure. Apparently some people come up with very imaginative ideas. A newly married couple drove a car showing WE 2 ARE 1. There's a story—I don't know if this one's true—that a man released from prison had a number plate 1 AM FREE. But my favourite is the elderly man whose old banger was practically falling apart and had the registration number MY LAST 1.

And on that same subject we found out something which surprised us. Whilst every vehicle has to display a rear number plate it is not compulsory in California to have also a front plate. Strongly recommended, but not compulsory. I can vouch for that because during our holiday, and especially when we were in the centre of L.A., I saw several cars without front number plates.

I think it was Chloe who first noticed that on American freeways there are no service stations such as we have on our British motorways. But they have far more exits than we have, much more frequently, and their signposting is absolutely brilliant. I don't see how anybody can possibly ever get lost in America. Plenty of signs and all with clear directions. Details of every town, every main road and showing the exact distance to the next exit.

We went past a school just as the youngsters were coming out and I commented that there did not seem to be any set uniform. Elizabeth's reply was that rules on what to wear in American schools are really no more than just general advice about styles of clothing. There is no pressure on anyone to wear specific uniforms and they have never come across the idea of a 'school colour'.

Mary remarked that there are two things you don't see on American roads—roundabouts and pedestrian bridges. I suppose they don't need roundabouts, which are a form of space-saver, because they have enough space to construct as many slip roads and flyovers as they wish. They actually do have a very few roundabouts (which they call circles) but only in the largest cities. I remembered that Maury had encountered some roundabouts during his visits to England and in his opinion the average American driver would have no idea what to do if he found himself at a roundabout.

And pedestrian bridges? Well, for a start, you need pedestrians. You don't get those in America. So there's not really any point in bridges.

I can't let this day go without telling you about a classic item in the newspaper. I always like to read local newspapers, wherever I go. That's where you really capture the true local atmosphere. And the one spot I always aim for is the page of Letters To The Editor. Apart from those that are witty, others are quite outspoken and vitriolic, even abusive at times. Great fun. Well, I saw one today in which the writer was blasting his fellow citizens for not standing up for their rights, for allowing bureaucrats to trample all over them. His final sentence was absolutely priceless—"Ask yourself, are you a pigeon or a statue?" I don't think I can possibly improve on the mental picture which that conjures up. I wish I had written it.

DAY 24

Catherine, Chloe and Emily had not yet seen the Pacific Ocean because Moorpark is a little way in from the coast. So that's where we took them today, with Phil in his by now customary position as driver. After a short journey along the freeway we turned off onto what in America is regarded as a minor road but nevertheless is still as good as some of our A-roads in Britain. This twisted and turned and very soon we were driving through the Malibu Canyon. Quite awe-inspiring, with mountains overhanging the road on both sides. It led us into the Santa Monica Mountains and when I say 'into' I really mean it. At one stage the road goes through a tunnel in the mountain. Emerging from it we then drove along a stretch where there is a steep drop on one side. At several points there are vantage areas, lay-bys where you can park in order to view the breathtaking scenery and take photographs—which we did, needless to say.

Eventually we got a glimpse of the ocean some way ahead of us. As we drew nearer we then passed some buildings set back from the side of the road on our right. This, we were told, is Pepperdine University. Americans claim that it has the most beautiful campus of any university in the world because on one side of it are these Santa Monica Mountains and on the other side is the Pacific Ocean. This university specialises in producing sports stars. That's something which we in Britain find difficult to understand. What they do at Pepperdine is accept as students those who are outstanding at athletics or sports and enrol them on courses which require very little academic work. It enables them to graduate, to qualify for a degree with hardly any effort. Meanwhile they can devote almost all their time to training without, as happens in other nations, having to sacrifice most of their leisure time. This gives the Americans a head start over other nations and helps explain why they tend to win far more honours than other athletes and sportsmen.

When we reached the ocean we then turned right onto the P.C.H. (the Pacific Coast Highway—remember?). After just a few miles we arrived at the Lee Carrillo State Beach, a spot which Elizabeth and Phil had discovered on previous drives. In spite of a blustery breeze it was comfortably warm and so we walked for some time. The water was a deep shade of blue but also a little on the rough side.

Quite a number of 'rollers'. Mary took some photos of these but somehow they don't look as impressive in a picture as they were in real life. We saw a number of birds which we wouldn't see back in Essex or Kent—slaty-backed gulls, sandpipers and pelicans. That reminded me of the well-known limerick:

A very strange bird is the pelican—
His beak can hold more than his belly can.
He takes in that beak
Enough food for a week
Though I'm blowed if I know how the hellican.

Do you know, in America even the birds seem larger than life. Everything, absolutely everything in the States is so HUGE.

Oh yes, we got a photograph of two flags flying backwards. Trust us to do that. You see, all along the Pacific coast there are coastguard stations every two hundred yards or so. There are trained lifesavers on duty throughout the day. In that part of the world the local people are extremely safety conscious. We came to one station with two flags flying—the Stars and Stripes and the Californian state flag. It looked like a good picture. But at the precise second that we clicked the shutter a strong puff of wind turned the flags momentarily the wrong way. Ah well, they do say that you can't win 'em all.

I referred to this as a state beach. In California a great many beaches are privately owned and thus the general public has no access to them. Those not in private hands come under the control of the authorities in Sacramento, the state capital, and are thus known as state beaches. So the word 'state' is a very important part of the name. From notices on display I saw that this beach is a recommended spot for scuba diving but we gave that one a miss.

Back in the car (sorry, the 'bus') we drove south along the coast heading for Malibu, which is a suburb of Los Angeles. We passed a roadside board proudly announcing '27 miles of scenic beauty'. That's because Malibu is sandwiched between mountain and ocean and over the years has grown by spreading along the coastline. And it really is beautiful. Not just the scenery but also the properties. Superb examples of architecture and brilliantly positioned on hillsides or overlooking the beaches. Many stars of screen and sport have made their homes here. As we drove along we were taking in the marvellous views previously enjoyed by Ronald Coleman, Barbara Stanwyck, Clara Bow and Jack Warner. More recent residents have included Larry Hagman, Dustin Hoffman, Demi Moore, Madonna, Robert Redford, Steven Spielberg, Sylvester Stallone, Tatum O'Neal and John McEnroe. How's that for a star-studded electoral roll?

Back home in the evening I was reading an article in the local paper about the increasingly litigious attitudes in American society. For example, the father of a schoolboy who had been playing in his school football team. After they lost four games in a row the sports master made a few changes and this boy was one of those now left out of the team. Immediately his father sued the school. The grounds for his action were that (a) the teacher's decision would undermine the boy's self-confidence; (b) this would seriously jeopardise his chances of success in the forthcoming exams; (c) therefore he would be unlikely to gain a place at university; and (d) the lack of a university education would make it unlikely that he could build a successful career in adult life. The father's argument was that the teacher was behaving in a way which could easily cause lifelong damage to the boy. So he was asking the court to order that his son be immediately and permanently reinstated in the football team regardless of match results.

At this point the case was still ongoing and so I do not know the outcome. However, the article also mentioned a case where a lady won compensation for sexual discrimination. For many years she and her husband, happily married for thirty years, had been loyal workers for their local branch of a national charity. The husband, in fact, was the branch secretary. Any correspondence from the charity was always addressed to them as Mr. and Mrs. So far so good. But came the day when the wife was elected as branch president. She demanded that all the charity's records, both national and local, be altered to show Mrs. and Mr. on the grounds that president is senior to secretary. When nothing was done she lodged an accusation of sexual discrimination and issued a writ against the charity. Her local court threw it out, saying that there was no case to answer. So she appealed to the Supreme Court in her home state. They overruled the previous verdict, ordered the charity to amend every record and awarded her very substantial damages, tens of thousands of dollars. What surprised me, though, was the judges' decision that part of the compensation be paid personally by her husband as he is an authorised official of the charity. I wonder what that has done for their thirty-years marriage.

To my way of thinking there is something terribly sad about folks who rush to the nearest court of law over the tiniest, slightest little problem. Tell me, whatever happened to goodwill, whatever happened to discussion and compromise? I must be getting old.

DAY 25

The remainder of this holiday would mostly be spent in L.A. and as there is a difference between Los Angeles and Los Angeles County perhaps I'd better explain the geography. I'll do it by making a comparison with London.

Central London includes districts such as Hammersmith, Lambeth and Islington. If we extend the area to *Greater London* we can then include places like Walthamstow, Dagenham and Kew. Similarly when we talk about Los Angeles we take in Hollywood, Beverly Hills, Long Beach and Santa Monica. *Los Angeles County* is a much bigger area and includes districts such as Malibu, Anaheim and Pasadena. But the distances involved are quite different in the two countries. L.A. County's population is just over one third of Greater London's yet it covers about four times the area.

Mary and I had already spent a day at Long Beach when we visited the Aquarium and the Queen Mary; yesterday Catherine and the girls saw Malibu. That had given us all a taste of the glitz and glamour of this part of California. Now today we were heading for one of the central spots—Santa Monica, the playground of L.A..

We parked on the promenade about a mile from the pier and walked towards it along the beach. That was easier said than done because our feet were sinking above the ankles in soft powdery sand and it became a bit tiring on the legs after a while. Along the promenade there is a pavement (sidewalk in American parlance) and side by side with that is an asphalt track about ten feet wide. This is used by cyclists, joggers and skaters which means that any pedestrians using it need eyes in the back of their heads. Santa Monica State Beach is superb and often used in films or in TV shows like Baywatch. As everyone knows, on any beach you can see how far the tide comes in by the lines of seaweed. Between the lines on this beach and the promenade is almost half a mile of this soft white sand. And it was quite warm to walk on because the temperature was round about 90 that day. Mary wanted a photo to show just how vast this beach is and so she stood at the water's edge facing inland across the beach. She paused there for a moment whilst the rest of us carried on walking. Because she was concentrating on getting a good picture she didn't notice a big 'roller' wave coming in.

Suddenly there was a great *SHOOOSSH*, she was drenched up to the knees and the frothy surf crashed onto the beach around her.

"Oh, dearie me," said Mary. (Well, that's a rough translation of what she said.) I'm sure you'll understand that we were all terribly sympathetic towards her. Practically doubled up with sympathy we were. As Phil remarked, "When you get back to England you can boast that you've paddled in the world's greatest ocean even if it wasn't exactly what you had in mind." And actually the weather was so hot that within about five minutes her legs and feet were quite dry again.

We ate a picnic lunch on the beach near one of those coastguard stations which I have mentioned earlier and while we were there two lifesavers arrived to start their spell of duty. Young Chloe and Emily went across to ask, "Can we have our pictures taken with you?" The two men were quite happy to oblige, made a big fuss of them and the girls were over there for almost a quarter of an hour. I think this was another example of what we had been finding, of Americans being fascinated by our English accents.

Then after lunch we made our way to Downtown. That's what Americans call every town centre in the same way as Main Street is their name for what we Brits call a High Street. Our British 'man in the street' is known in the States as Man on Main Street. And old fogies like me can remember Petula Clark going to the top of the charts with a song entitled *Downtown*.

Along the way we passed some beach shelters and it was obvious that the people sitting there were 'down and outs'. That prompted a discussion about wealth and poverty. In Britain there is growing concern about the steadily increasing gap between rich and poor, between the haves and the have-nots. But the situation is much worse in America. Although California is the richest state in the Union it also has the largest gap in the world between the very rich and the very poor. And the widest income disparities are in this Los Angeles area. It has come about because over the past twenty to thirty years there has been a catastrophic decline in the wages paid to unskilled workers. One political leader has declared that California is now two states. One is educated, satisfied and safe. The other is young, immigrant, uneducated (many do not speak English), restless and impoverished. I was taken aback when I heard that almost a third of the homeless in California are under the age of 18. And it seems that they have a big problem with illegal immigrants, coming over the border from Mexico. Catherine and her family know a thing or two about illegal immigrants, living as they do in Kent not all that far from Dover. But somehow we had not expected that California would have the same problem. Compare that with all those glossy travel agent brochures advertising the 'golden state'.

Mary and I had wanted to see the real America. In truth we were only seeing half of it. Back in Maryland Maury, a few years older than me, had been editor of the local daily newspaper until his retirement. That's why he knows everybody in town and everybody knows him. All his children are building professional careers—accountancy, law, education, childcare, scientific research. Then here in California Phil's career is going very well and he openly admits that he and Elizabeth live in an affluent part of Moorpark. So whilst we were having a great holiday in America we were doing so in the company of people who are financially secure. Poverty and all its horrors were a comfortable distance away.

After leaving the beach we spent a couple of hours meandering in a wide semi-circle through the main shopping centre, arriving back at the beach by the entrance to the pier. In all honesty it was much the same as any other shopping centre but for our new arrivals it was fascinating to see lots of familiar goods with strange price tags on them. "How much is that in our money?" Quite early in our holiday I had worked out a bit of mental arithmetic, a quick way of converting dollars into sterling. Not an exact conversion to the penny but near enough to give an approximate guide. So Mary started fielding all the questions from the girls with "Ask Grandad". Actually, this was just a continuation of the tenet she has adopted over many years and which seems to run along the lines of "I don't really see much point in marrying an accountant and then still doing sums myself". Gee, thanks.

In one pedestrianised area we saw something which we regarded as unpleasant. A man had a young monkey on the end of a chain and he was making the animal perform circus tricks. Sometimes when it was a bit slow he shouted at it or gave a fierce tug on the chain. We are a family of animal lovers and found the whole scene rather distasteful. There was quite a crowd watching but we only stayed for a moment or two and none of us put anything in the hat when it was passed round.

Then we joined the mass of humanity walking along the pier. You can't visit California without noticing the large number of Japanese people. L.A. in particular is a great magnet for them. We seven felt as if we were the only Europeans there, surrounded by Americans, Mexicans, Japanese and Canadians. There were lots of stalls with customers buying ice cream, postcards, kites, hot dogs, jewellery. Live bands playing folk or blues music. Some artists were writing people's names in very flowery calligraphy and Emily had her name drawn on a large sheet of card. This was America enjoying its Saturday off work in the sunshine. We stopped to buy some ice cream. By now I had become so confident at handling

American money that I even helped an elderly gentleman who was getting in a pickle with his small change.

I will always remember one man. From a distance it looked as though he was playing a row of chime bells. Because of the general hubbub we couldn't hear him until we got nearer when I realised that it was an unusual sound which I couldn't immediately identify. Then as we drew closer I saw the answer. They weren't chime bells, they were bones. All different sizes and lengths. It was so intriguing that in the end the others had to drag me away. I would happily have stood there for hours listening to that fascinating sound.

Then it was time to leave the pier and walk back to our 'bus'. We passed an area of beach which has been roped off and in it are row upon row of small wooden crosses. A notice tells us that there is one for each American serviceman and woman killed in Iraq. The area is now universally referred to as Arlington West. (It's because the Arlington National Cemetery is on the other side of the country in Washington. This display is, of course, on the west coast.) Whatever one's personal opinion on the rights and wrongs of America's involvement in Iraq I felt that this is a very calm, dignified and constructive way of honouring their memory. Very impressive and thought-provoking. Far more sensible than shouting slogans and waving banners.

Phil asked Mary, "Would you like to drive us home if I tell you the way?" Mary was horrified. "You CANNOT be serious!! What?? Sixty miles an hour along the freeway? In a strange car? With all those maniac drivers in the rush hour? And every single one of them driving on the wrong side of the road? You've GOT TO BE joking!!!" So Phil drove.

Considering that we had spent quite a large part of the day either on or next to the beach it was a coincidence that in the evening I read a magazine article about safe beaches. It was a report that a beach somewhere just north of Florida had been judged the safest beach in the world. I am not quite sure just what qualities they took into account in reaching that decision. The lowest number of accidents, maybe? Average weather conditions? Or the highest number of lifeguards per hundred yards? But what it did say was that their search involved checking every beach right down the Atlantic coast and then every beach down the Pacific coast. Hold on a minute—the safest beach in the world? What about all those around the Mediterranean? What about the marvellous beaches in, say, Australia?

Does the whole world consist solely of the U.S.A? Much as I like the Yanks this is a thought that crossed my mind more than once during these weeks.

DAY 26

Leaving Moorpark today we motored away from Los Angeles, heading northwest, and after an hour reached the small town of Ventura. Oh no, sorry, it's a city, isn't it? Everything's a city in California. First we went to the marina and what a lovely sight it was. It is quite large and there were literally hundreds of boats of all sizes and colours as far as the eye could see. Most of the quayside shops were open and as it was rather warm we headed towards an ice cream parlour. We were fascinated to find that the counter display was a long row of tubs, each with a different flavour of ice cream. I've never seen such a variety, even better than that selection we saw a week earlier in Thousand Oaks. When we had finally made our choices the assistant asked, "Do you want one scoop or two?" Fortunately we all asked for just one—fortunately because you should have seen the size of that one scoop. Crumbs, if we had asked for two I reckon we would all still be sitting there trying to get through it all.

As our party of seven included five females I suppose it was almost inevitable that they wanted to look around the clothes shops. Phil's eyes glazed over—I think he switched off—but I made an effort and adopted my "Yes, I am interested really" expression. But I must tell you about the sweater shop we visited. You know how they arrange all the racks in sizes—S, M. L. XL. Well, I could hardly believe my eyes when I saw a rack labelled 'XXL and Over'. Honest, there was a whole line of them. It just brings home what I have written about the size of Americans. Not all of them are gross but obviously there are sufficient like that for the shopkeeper to think it worthwhile carrying a considerable stock, enough to fill a whole rack.

At the far end of the marina we came to a building which is a kind of museum of the area with special emphasis on the marine and bird life. We were only in there for a short time but one point caught our attention. Posters advertising motorboat trips to a group of small islands just a short distance off the coast. These are called—guess what—the Channel Islands and are an absolute haven for wildlife. But what we were looking at was that these trips are also recommended as ideal for whale watching. What a pity that there were no sailings scheduled for this particular day.

It was approaching lunchtime and so we weighed up the options and decided that a Greek restaurant had an interesting menu. Bearing in mind the warm weather another point in their favour was that they had a few tables outside the restaurant as well as inside. So we had our meal sitting right next to the water. The food was excellent though the service was rather slow. Mind you, we probably didn't help matters seeing that all seven of us ordered something different.

After lunch it was back in the car and over to Downtown. In this part of California the most notable aspect is the impact of recent and continuing growth, almost consuming its once sleepy and agricultural past. But historic Ventura has managed to retain both its dignity and serenity. The Mission here was originally called the San Buenaventura Mission and is one of the better-preserved Missions. And just across the road we found the city museum with lots of paintings, carvings and historical artefacts.

Our collections of photographs now include quite a number from that afternoon in Ventura. It's because we were entranced by the variety of palm trees growing right there in the middle of all this modern activity. And citrus trees. And cacti. Yes, growing happily in the middle of Main Street.

For Catherine, Chloe and Emily this was their fourth day in America. They had long since recovered from jet lag and were now eagerly looking at and noting every detail of this new world. They asked, for example, why the letters C.P.O. are painted on some roads. Elizabeth explained that it stands for Car Pool Only. You may remember that while Mary and I were in Washington we had seen the letters H.O.V.—High occupancy vehicles, cars carrying more than just the driver. There are lanes on some freeways there which a driver cannot use if he or she is travelling alone. Well, over in California C.P.O. means exactly the same restriction.

On the journey back home we saw a caravan and Mary remarked, "That's the first caravan that we've seen in America." Phil replied, "Oh, they don't call them that over here. They are known as R.U.V's. It stands for recreational use vehicle."

I'm beginning to suspect that in order to speak American you have to be fluent with initials. We have already come across—

H.O.V.	high occupancy vehicle
C.P.O.	car pool only
S.U.V.	sports utility vehicle (our 4 x 4 people carrier)
R.U.V.	recreational use vehicle

Just before we reached Moorpark again a stretch limo passed us. Is it worth mentioning that, you may wonder? Yes, it is. Around the world California has the reputation of being the land where everybody drives a stretch limo. So you may be amazed to learn that during our five weeks in the States we only saw three of them. They really are a rarity. In fact, I've seen just as many since we arrived back in England. I suspect that here in Britain the fashion is developing for them to be hired as wedding cars. But believe me, you certainly don't see one on every street corner in America. No, not even in the Hollywood area.

By the time we reached home in the early evening we were all feeling quite tired. So a quiet day tomorrow was needed. Especially as we would be off to Disneyland on the following day. The girls were excited by this prospect. They have visited Euro Disney in Paris but this one in Los Angeles, the original one, is much bigger. So in preparation for that a bit of recharging of batteries was called for.

DAY 27

We had had three energetic days in succession and the next principal item on the agenda was Disneyland. So before we moved on to that it seemed clear that a quiet relaxing day was called for, a chance to draw breath. Phil offered to drive us around a bit more of the local area in the morning because the scenery there is quite stunning, a combination of mountain, valley and ocean. After a while we stopped at one of those outdoor barbecue sites where there were also facilities for beach volleyball, basketball and tennis. He produced his own basketball which he had brought along and we all messed around on the outdoor court taking shots at getting the ball into the net. (Hey, hold on, I thought this was supposed to be a quiet relaxing day!) Phil was very good at it because he has been playing basketball since living in America. Then Chloe left everyone except Phil standing—she plays a lot of netball at school and has a good eye for that type of sport. The rest of us were pathetic, and that's being complimentary.

Arriving back home Elizabeth had a couple of letters to post and this led to an explanation of the American post box system. They don't have letterboxes in the front doors of American homes. Instead for every half dozen or so houses there is one large box on a stand at the kerbside which comprises half a dozen small boxes, each with its own lock. So only the householder with the appropriate key can open his own box and collect his mail. Nearby, also at the kerbside, is another box. But this one has a little red flag on it and is just a straightforward collection point where you post your outgoing mail. It is also locked and the mailman (postman to you) has the key. I suppose the thinking behind all this is that he doesn't have to spend hours walking up and down people's front driveways. He only needs to walk along the pavement (sorry, sidewalk). It's so much quicker, and therefore saves on wages.

While Elizabeth sorted out lunch Phil was sitting at the computer, just generally browsing. He often does that and I asked whether it was expensive to use the computer for long periods. But he reminded me of two points. Firstly, computer usage is charged at local call rates and secondly, in America all local phone calls are free of charge. You only have to pay for long distance or international calls. So you can tap away at the computer all day long for free.

In the afternoon Elizabeth, Catherine and I paid another visit to the supermarket and while they were otherwise engaged I had a quick look around the confectionery aisle. I was interested to see several familiar names among all the Yankee sweets. Twix, Kit Kat, Snickers, Wurther's Original, M and M, they were all there. And one thing I have found out is that not every American is addicted to coffee. Most, but by no means all. So this afternoon I was also pleased to see packets of Earl Grey tea on display. But on the other side of the coin it does seem to me that most of their bacon is streaky, not the nice lean rashers which we are used to.

Oh, I learnt a new word this afternoon. Airhead. Elizabeth told me that it means 'idiot'. Two young women were having an argument because one of them had purchased a wrong item. The other one furiously called her an airhead. I think it's a superb word. Doesn't it conjure up exactly the right picture?

We decided to go out for a meal this evening. Elizabeth and Phil said, "We know just the place—it's at Simi Valley and is called Hometown Buffet. You pay a set price and can eat as much as you like." That sounded a bit too good to be true and we wondered what was the catch as we all piled into the bus and set off. But believe you me, there wasn't any catch. It was absolutely true—eat yourself to a standstill. I've never seen anything like it

When we arrived in early evening the place was already packed out and we joined a group of about twenty people who were queuing at the entrance. So it meant a wait of almost half an hour. The inevitable happened. As we chatted among ourselves others overheard our English accents and soon it seemed that everyone wanted to talk to us. I think that Chloe and Emily were amazed that they were suddenly the focus of attention.

Finally we got inside this self-service restaurant. The adult charge is the equivalent of about twelve pounds in our currency, there is no time limit on how long you stay and you can literally help yourself to as much food as you wish. How on earth do they make enough profit to stay in business? It must surely be something to do with the volume of turnover—the place holds about 200 customers and I am told that it is quite full throughout the day. But I do have one complaint. A notice announced that there is a reduced charge for holders of American Senior Cards. So I said to the cashier, "I am from England. It means that I don't have an American card but I can show you evidence that my wife and I are British senior citizens." But it didn't get me anywhere. "No, the discount is only available to American seniors." So I had an extra slice of roast beef to get my own back.

It was almost dark when we eventually drove back to Moorpark and again the girls were spotting things which I had not previously noticed. For a start the cats' eyes in the roads seem much brighter than the ones we have in England. We decided that the explanation is that the American ones must be set slightly more proud into the road than our own back home. And in the built up areas there appear to be fewer streetlights than in our English towns. But against that the Americans have the good idea of illuminating their street names. Now why hasn't anybody in Britain come up with a simple idea like that? It makes motoring after dark so much simpler.

An early night tonight for all of us. Tomorrow is the start of a three days expedition to Disneyland.

DAY 28

At last we had reached what Chloe and Emily were eagerly anticipating as the highlight of their Californian holiday. We were travelling to Disneyland today where we had booked rooms for two nights at the huge Disneyland Hotel. It's a two hours journey from Moorpark and so while we're travelling along let me tell you an amusing story about the beginning of Disneyland. (Though I'm sure the locals didn't think it was in any way amusing at the time.)

In the early 1950's 76 acres at Anaheim in the southern part of L.A. were selected for a theme park to celebrate the life and work of Walt Disney. Thus it was the Disney Corporation who introduced to the world this concept of the theme park where you pay a sizeable fee to get in but thereafter all activities and rides are free. There were a great many trees on this site—it was largely but not entirely orange groves. Already in those days there were a few serious environmentalists in high places and so a detailed arboreal study was carried out and decisions made on which trees to preserve. Then the architects did their work, planning everything very carefully so as not to disturb those trees. The final step was to tie ribbons around every tree on the site—red ribbons indicating which ones should be cut down and green identifying which should be left standing.

On 21 July 1954 the demolition company moved in and started to clear the site. As they went about their work they may have noticed ribbons on the trees but nobody had thought to tell them that these had any special significance. So in they went with their bulldozers and excavators and quite literally cleared the site. Flattened everything. Months of meticulous planning went straight out of the window. That's the type of thing I sometimes refer to as the left-hand / right-hand disease.

Nevertheless Disneyland was ready to open in 1955 and has always called itself The Happiest Place On Earth. It has been such a great success that there are now imitations operating around the world. It's interesting to reflect that while building work was in progress one opinion was that "It will be spectacular—a spectacular failure". But as I sit writing this the number of visitors so far is approaching 500 million!! It is much larger than those original 76 acres. Most of that is now covered by Disneyland Park but the area was extended to add a second part known as California Adventure Park. Those two together make up Disneyland, the part you pay to get into. Then in later years a third area has been built, Downtown Disney, but there is no entry fee for this. It's open for any local residents and casual visitors.

Disneyland Hotel is on the edge of Downtown Disney and when we arrived in early afternoon it's just as well that they were not too busy because our booking in became a major undertaking. See what you make of this episode. When we had originally booked our rooms by phone the payment had been made quoting Elizabeth's credit card details. Then when we arrived at the hotel our three rooms had to be registered separately. For each room they need credit card details to cover 'incidentals' which will be recorded and charged to you when you finally book out. But we managed to confuse the issue. Elizabeth and Phil used his card to cover their room and for Mary and me I registered my card. Catherine used her card for herself, Chloe and Emily. Meanwhile the computer already had Elizabeth's details and so in total was showing four cards covering three rooms. The clerk could see what we had done but he couldn't make the computer understand. He called a colleague and in the end it took them more than twenty minutes to get the information correctly recorded. Goddam English tourists!

When Mary and I arrived in our room the first thing we saw was an enormous bed. I have already written about the King-size beds in those new American homes which we visited but this one was even bigger. A super-King-size bed. Was this really supposed to be just a double bed? And hotel rooms are always full of literature, aren't they? Local attractions and amenities, official notices about fire regulations and first aid procedures. But here in California I found something different. How's this for a welcome?

> *The construction of Disneyland Hotel meets Californian earthquake standards. Your main concern during an earthquake should be to protect yourself from falling objects. The actual movement of the earth is rarely the cause of injury.*
>
> *If you are inside, stay there. Do not run outside. Stay away from windows and do not use elevators.*
>
> *If you are outside stay clear of buildings and power lines. Do not smoke and do not light matches. Telephones should not be used immediately after an earthquake as the lines are needed foe emergency calls.*

Makes you stop in your tracks for a moment, doesn't it? Makes you feel somewhat helpless. Especially as our rooms were up on the seventh floor of this enormous hotel. It brings home that earthquakes are a fact of life in Los Angeles.

After a suitable pause for unpacking and freshening up we all re-grouped downstairs in the reception area (pretending not to notice the apprehensive glances from the duty clerk) and set off to spend the rest of the day in Downtown Disney. It is a huge expanse of shops, amusement arcades, wine bars and restaurants. Everything, yes everything, is absolutely saturated with the world of Disney. All the employees are referred to as 'cast members' and quite a lot of them dress up.

Prices are high. I'm told that many Americans mutter that "Mickey is a very greedy little mouse". I heard the comment three or four times from different people. For example, the sales tax in Disneyland appears to be ¾ % higher than anywhere else in California. Popular opinion is that the extra bit is retained by the company though I was not able to establish for certain whether that is a fact or just gossip.

The girls received a lesson in the American language concerning the word 'toilet'. We had to explain that the Yanks never use that word. In the privacy of the home it is always known as the bathroom, even if it doesn't actually contain a bath. But in public areas and buildings it is called the restroom. They were getting a little concerned when they couldn't see any signs indicating bathrooms.

After spending some time touring the shops our thoughts turned to food. This posed a problem as there were so many choices available from all around the world and it was difficult to reach a decision. Elizabeth, unfortunately, was feeling a little off-colour and so after the meal she and Phil returned to the hotel. The rest of us passed the evening investigating more shops and just soaking up this total Disney atmosphere.

When British people talk about visiting Disneyland they usually mean either EuroDisney in Paris or DisneyWorld in Florida. Only a minority of them travel across the States to the original, the only one correctly named Disneyland, in Los Angeles. All the clothes in the shops there have Disney characters displayed on them or the name Disneyland. But Catherine wanted something which included the name California as evidence that she has actually been there. It developed into something of a treasure hunt but I think she did eventually find a sweatshirt. Heaven knows how much it cost her.

Our final stop in the evening was at a café to get a drink. A cold one, not hot. I had already discovered that Disneyland coffee is not up to the usual American standard and as for their tea—not on your life. You can get a decent cup of tea in the States if you make it yourself but their cafes have no idea how to produce a pot of tea. The most glowing compliment I can pay to American mass-produced tea is to say that it is diabolical. And that's when I'm in a good mood.

When Mary and I got back to our hotel room we did something terribly un-American. We opened a window. It seems to be an instinctive reaction among Americans that they switch on the air conditioning without even thinking of opening a window. Are they maybe allergic to fresh air? We found that in our room the A.C. was already on and humming away. Suspecting that this might keep us awake we twiddled with the controls for a few minutes to no avail. The only way to quieten it down was to switch it off. So that's what we did and opened a window instead. Then when we clambered into that gigantic bed we kissed twice—firstly to say goodnight and then to say goodbye. Meet you back here in the morning.

DAY 29

One of the restaurants in Disneyland Hotel is Goofy's Kitchen and that's where we all met up this morning. Elizabeth, thankfully, was okay again after a good night's rest. Right from the very first moment it was obviously camera-clicking time. All the staff are dressed as Disney characters and willingly pose for endless photographs with the customers. Because they welcome visitors from all around the world they avoid any language problems by not saying a single word from start to finish. All their gestures and reactions are mimed and I think they do it brilliantly.

It was a self-service meal offering every type of breakfast imaginable. Over to one side Catherine noticed a man preparing omelettes and so we headed over there. He had side dishes of fillings—chopped ham, cheese, sausage, tomatoes, mushrooms, you name it. And the size of the omelettes—he must have been using at least two eggs for each one. Honestly, one omelette on its own was a substantial meal. And when it was my turn to choose various fillings I felt quite pleased that I remembered to say, "chopped tom–ay–does".

As we were at Disneyland for two days it seemed logical that we would spend today in Disneyland Park and tomorrow at the California Adventure Park. When I stepped up to the pay desk the man there instantly identified me as English (I wonder how) and wanted to start a conversation. He was clearly an admirer of Princess Diana. "When Prince Charles talked about marrying that Camilla why didn't your Queen step in and stop him?" I explained that there are various shades of opinion in Britain but we accept that Charles is old enough to make up his own mind. But this didn't really satisfy him and as I walked away with my tickets he was still going on about "when Charles wanted to marry Camilla the Queen should have kicked his butt".

We started our visit by taking a trip on the old steam railroad. This does a circular tour of the entire park and we could see how it is all divided up into eight separate 'lands', each based on a distinct theme. After that introductory ride we then wandered along Main Street U.S.A which features early 20th century shops. Look at these lovely names—the Blue Ribbon Bakery, the Gibson Girls Ice Cream Parlour, the Carnation Café, the Candy Palace and Candy Arcade and inevitably a Penny Arcade. Main Street U.S.A. leads from the Town Square by the main entrance to the Central Plaza in the middle of the park where there is a statue of Walt Disney. Children can have rides up and down the Street on a vintage double-decker motorbus or a horse-drawn streetcar or—a great attraction—the wobbly, bouncy Jolly Trolley. (No Dad, you can't. It's for the kids.)

Then we explored the zone called Frontierland. The early settlers, Indians, that kind of thing. In the middle of this area is a large lake which encircles an island though I'm not sure whether the lake is natural or man-made. A Mississippi paddle steamer named Mark Twain carries passengers around the island but we decided that that was a bit tame. As an alternative there are Davy Crockett canoes, each seating about 20, and we fancied paddling our way around the island. As we all got on I somehow became separated from the others and found myself sitting on the opposite side of the canoe from them. It's many years since I last did some canoeing but I reckon it's like riding a bike. It all comes back after about 30 seconds. The lady sitting immediately behind me seemed to know what she was doing and the two of us got up a steady rhythm in our part of the boat. But the man just in front of me was a right Wally. He hadn't got a clue. Three or four times he smacked his paddle heavily against mine. Never mind, it was all harmless fun and we got right round the island and back to the landing stage without capsizing. The island is called Tom Sawyer Island and is really an adventure playground complete with haunted caves, a suspension bridge and Fort Wilderness. I understand that in the summer of 1970 this island was seized by a group protesting against the Vietnam war. They raised the Viet Cong flag over the fort before being forcibly evicted.

We grabbed lunch before the eating-houses got too crowded and from the extensive menu I chose a sandwich. You would think, wouldn't you, that by now I should have learnt my lesson. The American idea of a sandwich is almost half a loaf. It's a good job we were not in any hurry to finish our lunch quickly.

Then we moved on to New Orleans Square. The official American sales patter is that after the Civil War the North and South lived together happily ever after in places like New Orleans. According to the myth former slaves and slave traders forgot the past and together concentrated on churning out jazz and soul music. In this spirit of harmony they created exotic cuisines and gracious lifestyles.

A dream world, you say? Yes admittedly, but you see, that's what Disneyland is. A dream world come to life. As we wandered through New Orleans Square two chains of blue beads descended from Heaven upon Mary and Elizabeth. Looking up we saw two men smiling and waving from a balcony. Apparently in the old days it was traditional in New Orleans to shower trinkets and jewellery on ladies during festivals and parades.

(Back in England I have read something more about New Orleans—something which Mary and Elizabeth didn't know. During the Mardi Gras festivals there it was accepted that ladies and girls did not wear a bra. Then when a necklace descended from the skies the recipient showed her thanks by quickly flicking up her blouse or tee shirt, thus offering a momentary glimpse of her assets. I assume that the practice has not yet spread to Disneyland.)

One feature that went down very well with me was the plentiful supply of live music. In Main Street U.S.A. there was the Dapper Dans barbershop quartet, we had the oom-pah-pah Disneyland Marching Band and then some genuine Dixieland jazz in the New Orleans Square. All great stuff.

But there's one thing you will not find in Disneyland. Churches. That's because Walt Disney was quite disillusioned by all the fighting in the world arising from religious intolerance. His life's aim was to make people happy and he believed that religion represented a divisive element in life. So—no churches or chapels.

Our next destination was Fantasyland. The entrance to this is across a drawbridge into Sleeping Beauty Castle. Walt Disney recalled that famous European castles were often huge and intimidating and he set out to make this one exactly the opposite. Gentle colours everywhere, shades of pink and blue tinged with gold leaf. There are lots of rides in Fantasyland and to my great delight adults are allowed on too. There's Peter Pan's Flight where you are carried in a flying galleon and look down on London at night before coming face to face with Captain Hook. There's a chance to ride with J. Thaddeus Toad as he test drives his new motor car Next you can sit with your own Caterpillar and journey down the rabbit hole to join Alice on her adventures in Wonderland. I particularly liked the Unbirthday Party and the March of the Cards.

For our favourite we unanimously voted for It's A Small World. This is a salute to the children of the world and features, among other items, the Eiffel Tower, the Taj Mahal and the Leaning Tower of Pisa. Models are displayed dancing and singing in a multitude of languages and the holiday traditions of many nations are portrayed. All that remained after that was a short ride on Dumbo the Flying Elephant and a few circuits on the King Arthur Carousel. Do you get the impression that I thoroughly lapped up this part of the day? Thank goodness I never bothered to grow up. I would have missed out on all this.

(On that particular point the Americans apparently have a saying—growing old is compulsory; growing up is optional. And you may have come across our

British equivalent—any citizen can grow up to become Prime Minister; anyone who doesn't grow up can be Leader of the Opposition.)

The final destination of the day was Toontown. This is in the style of a small American township of the 1930's and here we find the 'homes' of the Disney characters. They wander happily around the streets smiling, waving, posing for yet more never-ending photo calls. We were able to take photos of Mickey, Minnie, Pluto, Goofy, Donald Duck, Pinocchio and Chip 'n' Dale (the Chipmunks). And I think we assembled several autographs as well to go with the pictures.

We didn't realise how time was passing until two or three lights began twinkling and our stomachs reminded us that evening was approaching. So it was goodnight to Disneyland Park and back to Downtown Disney where the restaurants offered a wider range of options. It was only when we sat down that we realised how tired we were, having been on our feet almost all day. But it had been a lovely day and I think the two girls were walking on the clouds. They didn't want it to end.

DAY 30

I don't think it would be entirely accurate to dismiss this morning as a disappointment. But really, yesterday had been such a superb day that perhaps inevitably today had a slight tinge of anticlimax. California Adventure Park is part of Disneyland and included in the entry fee but it is completely different from Disneyland Park. Frankly it is much the same as hundreds of similar parks around the world, though admittedly very big. Lots of exciting and thrilling rides of all descriptions. And although there is certainly a Disney presence it is not waved under your nose all the time. Apart from in the shops, of course.

Breakfast in Goofy's Kitchen once again. Plenty of laughter and camera-clicking and another chance to get to grips with those unbelievable omelettes. Then, suitably fortified, we set off for another energetic day.

First port of call in the Adventure Park was a great big Ferris Wheel. I've never been much of a Ferris man myself but everyone else wanted to have a go. So I was the carrier pigeon, looking after the bags and coats while the rest of the team all whizzed up and down.

But only Phil was willing to try the next attraction, a scenic railway. One of the tallest I've ever seen, and halfway through the ride it loops the loop. So for about three seconds riders are actually suspended upside down in open cars. Phil thought it was great. Indeed, he had two rides before we insisted that he come away. Mind you, he's a Lancashire lad who grew up in the area around Blackpool and so he's had plenty of experience of seaside attractions.

Next we arrived at the Grizzly Peak Area with its Grizzly River Run. The posters invite you to 'roar down this white water raft adventure'. I was quite content to watch other people doing that. (Hey, I hope I'm not starting to sound like a grumpy old Victor Meldrew.) Mary also waited with me—let these younger ones do that kind of thing. They all loved it, especially the bits where they crashed through clouds of spray.

Then we had a family conference and the general consensus was that this adventure park was nothing very special. Let's get a bite to eat and then go back to Disneyland Park. We knew there was going to be a mini-parade of Disney characters around lunchtime and we made sure we were back there in time to grab a good vantage point. There is a snapshot of the seven of us sitting in a line along a low wall, all munching apples or bananas.

Afterwards in a small open-air theatre, holding about 200 audience, they were staging an abbreviated version of Snow White. Mostly just the songs, only a small amount of dialogue. It lasted around half an hour, was very well presented—plenty of comedy from the dwarfs—and we agreed it was a winner. Then we spent the next couple of hours re-visiting some of the places we had enjoyed so much yesterday. It gave us the opportunity to have one more go on some of the rides. Oh all right, I'll admit it—two more rides on It's A Small World which by now we had unanimously voted as definitely the jewel in the crown of Disneyland.

We knew that there was going to be a Grand Procession during the evening and it would have been lovely to have stayed on to see that. But Moorpark is quite a distance from Anaheim, which meant we had a long drive ahead of us. So after taking a few final photos we made our way back through Downtown Disney to the hotel. Gathering up our various bits and pieces we all went downstairs to reception to check out. Thankfully this was nowhere near as traumatic as checking in had been, though I'm sure I sensed a relieved smile on the clerk's face as we disappeared through the revolving front door.

A final thought on Disneyland. The whole set-up is marvellous and money has obviously been no object. It really is the last word in that style of entertainment. But seeing that it is so totally American in its whole presentation I find it ironic that many of the scenes and attractions are based on British stories. Snow White, Goldilocks, Toad of Toad Hall, Alice, Peter Pan, to name just some. Where would Walt Disney have been without our British characters to turn to?

And a final, final impression. Disneyland attracts thousands of visitors every single day and while they are there they eat and drink quite a lot. Yet the whole place is spotlessly clean all the time, even around the restaurants and snack bars and barbecue areas. Yes, there are plenty of rubbish bins (they call them trash cans) and an army of cleaning staff but what I noticed was the way in which visitors showed respect for what was there. It simply made the whole visit such a pleasant experience.

DAY 31

Phew. After three non-stop days we needed the chance for a breather, a quiet day when we could just slow down and get our breath back. Elizabeth needed to visit the supermarket to stock up in the kitchen but this time only Catherine and I went with her. I was a little surprised when Elizabeth bought some Blu-tack and said it was for the ornaments at home. She doesn't have a great many ornaments on her shelves and I had not realised that under each one is a tiny spot of Blu-tack to hold it in its place. It's the earthquakes, you see. The tremors may be so frequent that after a while we don't notice them any more but they are sufficient to dislodge any delicate trinkets.

In just three days' time we would be on our way back to England and so I took this chance to buy a couple of bottles of Californian wine. Yes, I know that back home we can pop down the road to Tesco and get similar wine there. But it's not the same as actually buying them in a Californian shop and taking them back across the Atlantic. That makes them special.

Some relaxed sessions at the pool table this morning. We were all slowly improving but Emily, the youngest in our party, beat the lot of us. Pool, snooker and billiards are all games which are very much to do with angles and it was obvious that Emily has a good eye for judging angles.

Meanwhile it was rubbish collection day and so Phil was busy putting out the wheelie bin. Chloe and Emily had already noticed what I mentioned to you earlier—that outside every property the house number is painted on the edge of the kerbstone. Phil explained to them that each wheelie bin has to be left right next to its own number and if this is not done the rubbish will not be collected. Another example of this rigid philosophy that 'rules is rules'. Oh, and talking of kerbstones—in America you'll see that lots of them are covered with red paint. This indicates No Parking. We in Britain use yellow lines painted on the road surface but Americans prefer red. And they say that lines on the road will become blurred or unclear after vehicles have frequently driven across them. It is quite true that many British drivers have pleaded successfully that yellow lines could not be seen at the places where they had parked. Americans overcome that defence by painting the lines where they will not be driven over.

After this we would only have two more complete days in California before our flight back to London and the girls wanted to buy some typical American clothes. So after lunch we were taken to a large shopping mall. While we were there we learned a new word. Blowout. I always thought it had something to do with either burst tyres or a huge meal and so couldn't understand why it was painted on two shop windows. But now I know differently. In America a blowout is a closing down sale. I suppose the thinking is that everything in stock has to be blown out of the shop.

I had half expected that we might be wandering around there for the whole afternoon but in fact after as little as two hours the girls had found and bought what they wanted. So as it was a pleasant afternoon we had a bit of a drive around the area before going home. As we went along we chatted about our impressions of this part of the States. Was it what we had expected? Well, that rather prompted the admission that none of us had quite known just what to expect. All the glossy brochures go on about the sea, the endless sunshine, the glamour, the razzmatazz. Of course there is plenty of all that. But what we had also been seeing were the mountains, the Moorish architecture, the cleanliness—and at this particular moment in history the tremendous friendliness towards anyone with an English accent. It was flattering that so many ordinary people clearly wanted to talk to us and we seemed to be so welcome wherever we went. But whilst they could understand us there had been a few occasions when we had difficulty understanding them. We noticed it mostly with girls, so was it something to do with the high-pitched young female voices?

And speaking of accents we commented on the American tendency to speak almost in shorthand. A Yank will never tell you that his birthday is on the twenty-third of August. He will say it is August twenty-three. Perhaps a more striking example is if he is giving you some road directions. A Brit will say, "Drive along London Road and then take the third turning on the left into Dorset Boulevard." Here it is in American—"Take London and make a left at Dorset." Exactly half the number of words.

We passed one stretch of road with lots of flowers and a couple of boards advertising a local company. We were told that in some areas a company will 'adopt' a road. It means they take responsibility not only for making it look attractive but also for the surface maintenance and upkeep. Well, I suppose the local authority are pleased because it saves them a few dollars. It's another form of sponsorship. Not quite the same as we have in England. With us we have firms who sponsor, say, a roundabout. They plant lots of flowers and accept responsibility for its upkeep. But they are not involved in any way with road surfaces.

Get to bed at a reasonable time tonight. Tomorrow the merry-go-round gets up speed once more. Never a dull moment when our family goes on holiday.

DAY 32

For Chloe and Emily the high point of the holiday had been the visit to Disneyland but for Catherine today was what she had eagerly anticipated. Today we were all off to Hollywood. A slight disappointment in that we wouldn't be able to tour the Universal Studios, but never mind—there must be plenty more to see.

Hollywood is quite close to the centre of Los Angeles. On previous visits to Malibu, the Getty Centre and Santa Monica we had not needed to go as far as the centre. By contrast Long Beach and Disneyland were away on the far side of the city and to reach them we had driven around Los Angeles, not through it. Today, however, we had no option but to plunge into the thick of the horrendous L.A. traffic. Believe you me, the quality of some of the driving in this city would maker even Postman Pat's hair stand on end. We aimed for Hollywood Boulevard which is reputed to be one of the most glamorous streets in the world. Our map indicated a large car park, Hollywood at Highland. That's the American way of saying "at the junction of Hollywood Boulevard and Highland Avenue". Another example of this speaking in shorthand.

Arriving there we found a massive multi-storey complex—perhaps I should call it arr-sm—with parking on various levels underground and the Kodak Theatre at street level. According to the publicity blurb there is also a 640-room hotel, a whole host of eating-places and 70 world-class retailers. The total cost of constructing all this was $ 385 million!

After parking our bus we took the elevator up to ground level and found ourselves at the entrance to the theatre. This Kodak Theatre is where they hold the famous Academy Awards ceremony each year. Catherine noticed a sign about conducted tours of the building. It wasn't clear whether or not any were scheduled for today and so she enquired from the girl at the ticket desk. The answer was, "The theatre is being used for a performance this afternoon and they are getting the stage ready. But there may be just enough time to fit in a tour now." I think that our English accents possibly influenced that decision. And a few other folks standing nearby also showed an interest in seeing the theatre. In the space of a minute or so here were a dozen customers eager to start and so another member of staff came along and offered to take us around straight away.

He was a likeable chap with a good sense of humour and an obvious enthusiasm for this building. I didn't make a note of his name but he told us that, like many L. A. residents, he often earns a few dollars by appearing in crowd scenes for the film companies. He rattled off the titles of several successful films in which he had taken part but obviously his name would never appear on the credits as he was only an 'extra'. First he led us into the main reception area. Deep pile carpet everywhere and gentle lighting. There is a bar at one end and he said that this is where those who are not 'special guests' can buy their drinks.

Then he led us through to where the privileged ones get their cocktails. It is the exclusive lounge known as the George Eastman V.I.P. Room and it has a really fascinating feature. The floor-to-ceiling double doors are entirely glass and from a distance you can see into the lounge. But as you draw nearer the glass mists up and you can no longer see through. I'm not technical enough to be able to explain it in detail but I assume that the glass is treated with some heat-sensitive coating. So you'll be disappointed if you hope to find out what is Harrison Ford's favourite tipple. Does this security system only work if you walk directly towards the doors? Not so. I tried creeping up on them from one side but they still misted up. However, we were allowed to step into this V.I.P. room and sample the lush armchairs for a minute or two.

Then we went into the main auditorium and what a sight greeted us. There is seating for 3,000 people on four levels and above everyone is what is called 'a tiara of light', an enormous oval chandelier. We were invited to sit in the very front row of the stalls. This is where the Oscar winners sit so that at the appropriate moment they can step up onto the stage and receive their awards. (And sometimes deliver lengthy cringe-making speeches.) Our guide had already been told that Elizabeth and I are musicians and so he pointed out the orchestra pit which looked rather more comfortable than some I have seen. He took us all upstairs so that we could see everything from one of the V.I.P. boxes—this is where the film directors, producers and similar gods watch the proceedings. Again we were allowed to sit where many famous bottoms had previously rested.

As we walked along various corridors we admired signed photographs of famous film stars. And there were also a number of Oscars on display—yes, the real ones, not imitations. It was all a fascinating insight into the film world and when we arrived back at reception we thanked our guide for taking us round at such short notice.

One thing surprised me. Out in the street above the main entrance are the words KODAK THEATRE. Note the spelling—I was expecting it to be THEATER. In several pamphlets about the Oscars I have seen it spelt in the American way but there on the very building right in the middle of Hollywood it has the British spelling. If you find that hard to believe we have photographs to prove it.

Outside there are numerous walkways in this Hollywood at Highland complex and they feature a lot of mosaics. These are large paving slabs on which individual stories are etched describing very briefly this or that person's film career. All very exciting and starry-eyed. This type of thing—

> "I came to Hollywood as a 17-year old from Kansas with just five bucks in my pocket. After two years as a street cleaner I was accepted into the back row of a chorus. After another two years I was humming a tune one morning when a famous producer overheard me and said I had a good sense of rhythm and pitch. So he gave me the leading part in his next blockbuster film."

Yes all right, I've just made up that story but it was the kind of C.V. we were reading. You know the idea, pathetic rags to unbounded riches in just three weeks (or in six months if you're unlucky). I found it quite amusing because it was all so unreal, so much a typical part of this make-believe world which is Hollywood.

Of course, what gives Hollywood Boulevard its special reputation is the large number of bronze stars set into the sidewalk. These are known as the Hollywood Walk of Fame. The idea started in 1960 with just eight stars but there are now nearly three thousand and each bears a famous showbiz name. As Catherine, Chloe and Emily have the surname Chaplin it was inevitable that when we found the Charles Chaplin star we had to have a snapshot of them crouching down next to it. They are not really related to him in any way but if we showed you the photograph you wouldn't have known that, would you?

A little way along the street is the Mann's Chinese Theater which was opened in 1927 by showman Sid Grauman. It is famous because the concourse in front of it is made up of concrete slabs. Whenever a film was premiered here the stars left their hand or footprints and signatures in the wet cement. To the younger ones in our group these were simply historic names but for Mary and me it brought back memories. I'm afraid we felt a bit ancient when we saw names of actors and actresses we remembered watching in the 1940's and '50's. Charles Laughton, Bette Davis, James Cagney, Clark Gable, Doris Day, Shirley Temple. But at the same time it also gave me once again that sense of a link with history which I had felt several times during these weeks in America.

And we saw what I suppose can be described as the Hollywood equivalent of busking. Nobody playing music in the streets such as we see in England but numbers of people strolling around dressed as famous stars or film characters. They are willing, indeed eager, to pose with you for photographs but in return they expect payment.

Naturally there are souvenir shops selling imitation Oscars and there are notices pointing out that the photographing of customers holding these Oscars is not allowed. Not actually illegal but seriously frowned upon. Well, we spotted one such shop where the staff were very busy with lots of customers. So Elizabeth primed her camera, I walked into the shop, picked up an Oscar, she immediately took just one shot and I replaced it on the stand. It was all over in about three seconds—we were both out of the shop and away up the road before the wrath of the management could descend upon us from a great height. I think it has turned out to be quite a good picture but on relating the story to others I have heard some maiden aunt-style mutterings about leading my daughter astray and not behaving like a responsible adult. But hey, hold on a minute—who on earth wants to go through life being always a responsible adult? Where's the fun in that? And anyway, it was her idea, not mine!

So that was Hollywood Boulevard, was it? Considering the massive hype which it gets I honestly found it a bit underwhelming. Just a very busy street packed with people and traffic, lots of shops and a few famous landmarks. One or two side turnings offer a distant glimpse of the famous HOLLYWOOD sign away on the mountainside. To give the girls a much better view of it we drove over to Griffith Park. For Mary and me this was a return visit but I'm glad we did it as I noticed something we had missed first time round. (Of course, on that previous day we had had one eye on the clock as we needed to get across town to the airport.)

Quite close to the observatory a special tree has been planted in memory of George Harrison, one of the Beatles. The inscription on a brass plate reads:

The George Harrison tree.

In memory of a great humanitarian who touched the world as an artist, a musician and a gardener.

"For the forest to be green each tree must be green."

I wonder if there is some story behind all this. Did George, as distinct from all of the Beatles, have some special link with Los Angeles? Is there some significance in the tree being planted at this particular spot? Since then, back home in England, I have tried doing a bit of research on the subject but with no luck so far. If there is a story, maybe I'll ferret it out one day.

Back in the centre of L.A. after lunch we spent a little time driving around the wide avenues of Beverly Hills. Here are the magnificent homes of Tinseltown's high and mighty. There are conducted tours available during which the guides will identify for you exactly who lives where but we didn't bother with all that. We were content just to admire the superb buildings—we weren't particularly bothered about who pays the council tax.

What Catherine particularly wanted to see was Rodeo Drive (pronounced roh-day-oh). Here are all the top-notch shops. I quote from a leaflet:

> *The Rodeo Drive legend is much bigger than the street itself. The most popular activities are window-shopping and people-watching. The shops are expensive but don't worry about looking out of place. Tourists abound, clad in off-the-rack fashions, gawking just like you will be.*

So that's what we did for a couple of hours. Window-shopping. Well after all, you should see the price tickets in windows of shops like Gucci, Tiffany, Versace, Dior, Cartier, Chanel and Saks. One shop is named Bijan—apparently you need an appointment just to get into the store and they claim that the average customer spends $100,000 (that's £70,000). So we contented ourselves with taking a few photos of each other standing *outside* some of these famous stores.

Young Emily is a great admirer of the American singer Britney Spears. Before leaving England she had scoured the internet and somehow discovered the name of the road in Hollywood where Britney lives. "It's the house at the far end of the road." We had a little time to spare before the journey home and so agreed to go and see the house. From our street map we found that the road is a turning off Sunset Boulevard which gave us an excuse to ride down this famous street. We turned into the relevant side road and drove along—and along—and along. It really was a very long road which finally ended in a cul-de-sac. Trouble was that there are two houses side by side at the end and so which one is Britney's? Both properties are 'gated' and both have numerous trees and bushes in front which severely limited our view of them. Ah well, we paused for a few moments, looked as best we could at both places and then made our way back. At least Emily can now claim she has actually seen Britney Spears' home even though we're not sure which one it was.

It had been quite an energetic day and by the time we arrived back in Moorpark and had a meal we were all ready to spend the evening sprawled on settee and armchairs. A basketball match was being televised and Phil did his best to explain the rules and all the subtleties as it went along. The impression I got was that you need to be at least six feet six tall to stand any chance in basketball. I found it fairly interesting but would much rather have spent the evening catching up on news of the English football season back home.

DAY 33

It seemed hard to believe that this would be our last full day in the States before flying back to England. The Iraq conflict was still monopolising the television news bulletins and reporters were appearing on screen with Washington's Capitol in the background. It was just over four weeks since Mary and I had been there, yet it seemed ages ago. We had packed so much into these weeks.

I don't think I mentioned to you that Elizabeth and Phil's house is at the top of a hill and this offers a superb view. But the down side is that their garden is on a pronounced slope and is thus not easy to control. For some time they had thought about getting it landscaped and now they had received some drawings. I suspect that Phil also had the ulterior motive of getting this professional help to beat those darned gophers. He spread out the drawings on the pool table and we passed the morning in packing ready for our flight, studying the drawings and consuming endless cold drinks.

I felt quite pleased with myself this morning because I had yesterday sent an e-mail to our son Andrew using an American computer. Just a brief message to confirm our flight schedule and to say roughly what time we would hope to arrive back in Southend. As Phil's life revolves around computers he has a very fine all-singing all-dancing state-of-the-art machine at home and had been kind enough to say to me, "Go on, help yourself. Send a message to Andrew." U.S.A. computers are very slightly different to British ones and so with fear and trembling I clicked the Send button and everything disappeared into the ether. Had I done all the right things and would the message ever see the light of day again? Well, when Phil switched on the computer this morning there was an answer for me. Of course, I had never doubted for one moment that I can handle American computers!

After lunch we all went for a walk in the mountains. That sounds a bit energetic, doesn't it? But it wasn't too bad really. Phil drove us to a spot in the foothills known as the Malibu Creek State Park. Leaving the car we strolled along an unmade road at the side of a stream and then gradually started to climb, but it was a fairly gentle gradient. After a few minutes two Park Rangers came along in a van, obviously on their routine patrol, and were quite happy for us to take photographs of them. In fact, looking back over the entire holiday, we never had a single instance of anyone being unwilling to be photographed. If anything, the one slight snag was that as soon as people heard our accents they all wanted to stop and chat with us. It had happened in Maryland but was especially noticeable in California, on the far side of America. I suppose there are not as many British accents over there on the west coast as there are in, say, Washington, New York or Florida. It certainly gave all of us that warm feeling of being welcomed by everybody.

Those two Rangers were the only people we saw throughout the couple of hours we were walking. It seemed so amazing that in the space of minutes we could drive out of a town with 100,000 residents and be up in the hills with not a building or a human being in sight. Absolute silence all around us on this brilliant sunny afternoon. Plenty of evidence of wild animals, though. This really was communicating with nature. Yet we were so close to Los Angeles, one of the largest and noisiest cities in the world. It certainly is true that California—and the southern part in particular—is indeed several worlds rolled into one. We were having the experience of a lifetime.

We had decided that getting films developed is cheaper in America than in Britain and so had left quite a pile of them at the local supermarket. We collected them this afternoon on the way home. That set the scene for our final evening. After clearing the dinner things away we spread photographs all over the table. The idea was to number them all and make lists of what each picture showed.

It turned out to be an Herculean task. I suppose that if we had kept at it the job might not have taken too long but I'm sure you can guess what happened. As we looked at various photos we started reminiscing about what we had seen and done. The talking eventually took far, far longer than the listing. So we were all quite late to bed that night.

DAY 34

I reckon there must be some law which dictates that the only way to pack a suitcase and then get it closed is for one person to sit on it. Well, that was the solution which Mary and I had to adopt this morning. I couldn't understand the reason why because the presents we were taking back to England were less in number that those we had brought out a few weeks earlier. One of life's insoluble mysteries. As the various items of luggage became ready we all placed them by the front door and throughout the morning the stack grew and grew. As I looked at it I had mixed feelings. We all know how lovely it is to return to one's own home and I was certainly looking forward to that. But at the same time these had been a brilliant five weeks and I felt a little sad now to be at the end of them.

I think everyone else felt the same way because as we sat eating our lunch it seemed that we were a little quieter than usual. Not so much of the normal bounce and chatter. Mind you, there might also have been an element of feeling a bit shattered. We had certainly lived life to the full in every minute of the holiday and probably needed to go home for a rest!

So after lunch we packed everything into the cars. Two cars this time—Elizabeth's as well. That was because after we had been deposited at the airport the 'bus' would have to be taken back to the hire firm and then Elizabeth and Phil would need her car to get them back home. So we were able to spread out. Mary and I travelled with Phil and the others went with Elizabeth. We got separated a little way before the airport because Phil was required to return the vehicle with a full tank of fuel and so we stopped at a garage. While he was standing there by the pump a very scruffy man ambled up to him. I couldn't hear what was said but Phil shook his head and the man wandered across to another customer. It turned out that he was asking for money. I suppose that while a driver is standing by a petrol pump he is a kind of captive audience. Phil told us that this type of begging is a daily occurrence in Los Angeles.

We all finished up at the car park immediately opposite Terminal 1 at the airport. You will recall that when we had gone there to meet Catherine, Chloe and Emily I had not been very impressed with the arrivals area of Terminal 1. A bit dowdy. Well, it turned out that the departures area was just as grim. Rather subdued lighting, a distinct shortage of seating, it all gave a somewhat gloomy impression. Even the snack bar we found was, shall we say, basic. Then after saying goodbye to Elizabeth and Phil we made our way through the various checkpoints. We were now almost on the point of leaving America but there was still enough time left for me to upset the U.S. Customs officers.

What happened was this. They had one of those screening machines which you walk through and it bleeps if it identifies any metal. When it was my turn I took out of one pocket my loose change and put it in a bowl which the officer was holding. Thank you, sir. I then stepped forward, BLEEP. Oh silly fool, I had forgotten the bunch of keys in the other pocket. I put those in the bowl with the money. Try again, sir. I stepped forward. BLEEP. At this point two other Customs officers started to take an interest and came across to us. One of them carried a type of baton which had a metal detector tip. He held it in front of me and I noticed that at this stage they stopped calling me 'sir'. It bleeped when he held it next to the breast pocket of my jacket. Well, all I've got there is my spare pair of glasses in a case. I handed it to him and he made a big show of removing the glasses and thoroughly examining the case. He found nothing and so passed the baton over me again. When it reached the breast pocket—BLEEP. By now I was starting to find the whole business rather tedious but I kept my cool. You don't get upset with Customs officers who seem to think that they are on to something.

But what on earth was the attraction about the breast pocket? Feeling a trifle bemused by now I felt inside it and suddenly realised the answer. Apart from just one day I had dressed in casual clothes for the whole holiday. The exception was that day when we went to the White House. Then I dressed smartly, including a shirt with cuff links. Later when the shirt was washed I removed the links, slipped them into the breast pocket of my jacket and had forgotten all about them until now. I produced them with a weak apology. Stern faced the officer waved the baton just once more—it bleeped in front of my stomach but that was the buckle on my belt. He admitted defeat but one other officer insisted on frisking me before they handed back what was in the bowl and let me continue on my way. To the relief, I suspect, of the other passengers who had been waiting behind me with mounting impatience.

Well, I reckon it was quite an achievement. I've actually been frisked by American Customs officers. That's one up on Mary. All she can claim is that she had her handbag searched at Heathrow.

Our flight was announced, all the boarding formalities went smoothly, we settled into our seats and the aircraft took off on time. Actually it was ten minutes late but that's 'on time' in aviation language. So here we go. It was dark by now and as we climbed into the night sky our final view of Los Angeles was the brightly illuminated Santa Monica pier.

Au revoir, America.

DAY 35

I suppose we could have an endless debate as to exactly when Day 35 began. You see, we took off from Los Angeles in mid-evening Pacific Time and flew for almost eleven hours. When we landed at Heathrow it was early afternoon Greenwich Time. Along the way we had flown through seven other time zones. So when exactly did we pass at midnight from one day to the next?

I'll admit that I took the easy option. As soon as we were in the air I put my watch forward eight hours and went through the whole journey on British time.

For the first half of the flight it was nighttime and we followed our route on the in-flight screen. We went roughly north-easterly across the centre of the States, passing over Las Vegas, Denver and Kansas City before eventually meeting the Atlantic a little way north of the Canadian border. We had only been airborne a short time when they served the evening meal. Yes, you're quite right—chicken. (You're getting the hang of it now, aren't you?) In all fairness I must say that the food was quite reasonable. My only gripe about airline meals is that the cabin staff are very busy and tend to want you to eat up as quickly as possible. I don't think I'm a particularly slow eater but I do like to enjoy my food. I don't want to gobble it down.

I would estimate that in our section of the aircraft there were around 70 to 80 passengers. As time passed seat lights were being switched off one by one. Emily fell asleep in a very short time and I think Catherine did as well but Mary and I were wide-awake. We read, we watched the in-flight programme, we chatted. By the time we had been flying for some four hours no more than a dozen people were still awake.

Sitting there quietly my thoughts wandered back over these past weeks. How lucky we were. We had seen some of the usual tourist sights—Pennsylvania Avenue in Washington, Malibu, Disneyland, Santa Monica beach and pier, the Queen Mary, the Getty Centre, Hollywood, Santa Barbara. We had also visited that marvellous pumpkin farm and the Indian pow-wow—two events which tourists would not normally know about. We had chatted, in his private office, with a young businessman who has already banked his first million and is well on the way to his second. We had spoken, momentarily, to the Vice-President of the

United States. There was the big party with Maury and Mary's family and also that barbecue with the Girl Scouts and their families. Two occasions when we were surrounded by lots of ordinary everyday Americans. And we had been so privileged to see parts of the White House and the Capitol which the vast majority of people, including Americans themselves, could never expect to see. A truly memorable holiday. We had been so wonderfully, incredibly lucky.

Those who were asleep, or those whose seats were away from the windows, missed a marvellous experience. Something which Mary and I will remember for many, many years. We were out there in mid-Atlantic when dawn broke. Over a period of, say, a quarter of an hour the black sky perceptibly changed to a dark grey. Then away on the horizon we saw a pencil-thin line, first a sort of dull cream and then slowly turning white. Looking carefully we could just make out the tiniest, slightest deviation from an absolutely straight line. We realised that because we were flying at a height of nearly seven miles we were actually seeing the curvature of the world's surface.

A hostess was moving around offering water to the few who were awake. "Enjoying the view?" she asked as she filled our beakers. "This is absolutely spellbinding," we replied. "This is easily the best part of the whole journey." Gradually the dull sky became brighter, that white line grew wider and at the same time changed from white to orange, from orange to gold. Then finally the tip of the sun appeared, slowly rising from beyond the horizon. Within another quarter of an hour we were looking out at a bright sunny morning. Magic it was, sheer magic. It's in moments like this that Nature makes mere human beings feel totally insignificant

During the holiday we had been practically starved of British news. However, from weather reports of leading international cities we knew that the average temperature in London had been some thirty degrees cooler than California. "You'll notice the difference when you get back to England," everyone had told us. And we had also seen frequent mention of rain. Today it remained bright sunshine until we were flying over Northern Ireland at which time the pilot took us down to a lower flight path and we then had sunshine above us and grey clouds below.

We flew over the mainland coast a little way south of Glasgow, continued inland for a while and then turned to fly south down the centre of the country passing near Birmingham and Oxford. Periodically the pilot reduced height; as he did so we flew into more cloud and before long there was rain on the windows. Oh joy, we're back in England!

We could have, we should have, landed at Heathrow on time. We were ready. But there was congestion—possibly the bad weather was slowing things down slightly. So we had to circle round for about twenty minutes until we got clearance to land. Inevitably some passengers then erupted in a frantic scramble to get off the aircraft, grab their baggage and rush through Customs. I accept that they possibly get away from the airport four and a half minutes before I do but I often wonder just why they do it. What do they achieve by 'winning' four and a half minutes? What do they do in those minutes to enhance the quality of their lives? Are they any more relaxed, any happier than I am? Meanwhile our family group in our own good time found a couple of trolleys, collected all our luggage and waved our passports at an Immigration officer who appeared to have only a passing interest. Then as we walked through to the crowded main reception hall we saw Andrew and Paul signalling to us, doing what could have been mistaken for impressions of a couple of hysterical windmills.

To drive Mary and me back to Southend Andrew would be using the northern half of the M 25. But to take the others home to Kent Paul would use the southern half. He had already heard that a major accident was causing problems on that southern section and so was anxious to make a start without delay. We all said our goodbyes after which Andrew, Mary and I went in search of a snack bar. I was quite happy to drink a coffee standing up after having sat for some eleven hours.

Before long we were on the final stage of our lengthy journey and it was back to reality with a bump. Do you know of anything more romantic than crawling along the M 25 in heavy traffic with the rain pelting down? Andrew told us that there had been some serious flooding around the country while we were away. After our experiences of five-lane freeways the three-lane motorway seemed almost claustrophobic. But when we eventually reached the Southend borough boundary it was nice to see familiar sights once more.

A neighbour had been keeping an eye on the house for us and had gone in each day to pick up the post. He left it in a pile next to the telephone. Crumbs, what a load of old toot we all get in the course of a month. Have you noticed? I'll sort this lot out in the morning. Too tired now. We had a light meal and both felt ready for an early night. Yes, I know it was only early Tuesday evening but we hadn't slept since Monday morning during which time we had gone through two busy days and travelled five and a half thousand miles.

After breakfast the next morning the first priority was to go over to the cattery where we got a tremendous reception from our two mogs. After I had paid the bill my wallet didn't feel very well but it was an exceptionally good cattery and we knew they had been really well cared for. Nevertheless they were obviously over the moon to be with us back home again.

Back home again. Yes, it was all over now. Just a memory. History. Once the long winter evenings arrive we will put all those photos into albums. (Should that be alba? My Latin's getting a bit rusty after all these years. I know that the plurals of stadium and medium are stadia and media.) Then I'll settle down to writing it all up as a story. The story of a lifelong dream which actually happened.

If you don' have a dream how you gonna have a dream come true?

978-0-595-39216-2
0-595-39216-4

Printed in the United Kingdom
by Lightning Source UK Ltd.
121940UK00001B/163-192/A